India's Energy Security

India's Energy Security

by

Lt Col Vivek Dhall

(Established 1870)

United Service Institution of India
New Delhi

Vij Books India Pvt Ltd
New Delhi (India)

Published by

Vij Books India Pvt Ltd
(Publishers, Distributors & Importers)
2/19, Ansari Road
Delhi – 110 002
Phones: 91-11-43596460, 91-11-47340674
Fax: 91-11-47340674
e-mail: vijbooks@rediffmail.com

The views expressed in the book are of author and not necessarily those of the USI or publishers.

CONTENTS

FOREWORD

Over the years, energy security has assumed vital importance for a country like India with widening gap between demand and supply of all sources of energy viz. coal, oil, gas and nuclear etc. A significant part of the country's energy requirements are met through imports. Our economy is thus susceptible to vagaries of international price movements with its resultant negative impact. Higher imports with inevitable large outgo of foreign exchange and the attendant Current Account Deficit has direct repercussion on country's economy and its overall development.

India is the fourth largest economy in the world and is expected to grow more than 5-6% per annum in the coming years. Besides it is the fifth largest energy consumer accounting for around four percent of total annual energy consumption. Our population of more than one billion people which is constantly growing will ensure that India remains one of the largest energy consumer and a net energy importer. Energy is the key ingredient for economic growth and for improving the quality of life.

Apart from increased energy requirement in view of our growing population, there is another allied factor namely energy intensity which has direct relationship with energy requirement. Energy Intensity refers to the energy consumed per unit of GDP growth. Our intensity is double than most of the developed countries. This is due to inefficient use of energy be it in industrial agricultural or transport sector. There is a greater need for demand management as 'Energy saved is energy produced.

It is with this background that we have to give the highest attention to ensuring "Energy Security"for country both in long term and short term." Energy Security" does not mean "Energy Independence". 'Only few countries are fortunate to have abundant resources of energy. Most major economies like USA, Japan, Brazil and India have to depend upon imports to meet their energy requirements to varying degrees. In this global context, it is all the more necessary for India to make comprehensive plans for its "Energy Security"particularly over long term.

Lt. Col VivekDhall has made a very detailed and in- depth research in the form of a well-documented book on India's Energy Security. He has made a very comprehensive coverage of all aspects and sources of energy and has come up with useful suggestions. The book deals with all issues of energy procurement including geopolitical pressures, transportation problems, vulnerability of international transit routes due to risk of terrorist attacks, piracy natural disasters and inter country disputes. He has highlighted existence of international choke points and their impact on free flow of energy resources. This book will be of good help to the policy makers in the government.

J S Oberoi

Convener, Energy Think Tank

Preface

Energy is an essential ingredient for social development and economic growth. Achieving the goals of poverty eradication, improved living standards and increased economic output imply increasing energy requirement. It has been estimated that by 2031, India's energy needs would be about seven times that of 2001 levels. The current trends in oil and gas production, and the level of coal reserves clearly indicate that the country will face constraints in indigenous availability of conventional energy resources. This coupled with widening of gap between energy demand and supply means increasing and higher levels of energy imports. It is estimated that India's fossil fuel import dependence will reach about 80% by 2031. Such a trend obviously militates against energy security apart from adversely affecting the overall economy.

The purpose of this book is therefore to bring together a set of opinions and analysis with a view to crystallizing the assessment of challenges and opportunities before the nation on a subject that will remain central for some time to come. India's energy concerns are really in the midst of a perfect storm: growing import dependency and rising prices of the fuels that the country needs to import; the complex geopolitics around energy supply sources and growing pressures of the global community to make emerging economies, including India accept commitments to limit the emission of greenhouse gases. In many ways, these forces should create. The key objective of this book is to highlight the internal and external dimensions of India's energy security scenario, the choices it is consciously making and the room to maneuver that it possess in which to address these concerns.

Acknowledgements

I would like to place on record my gratitude to the United Service Institution of India (USI) for accepting my research proposal and providing a congenial and conducive environment to do my research. My special thanks to Major General Y K Gera (Retired) who is the consultant (Research) at the Centre for Strategic studies and simulation at the USI and who was most encouraging throughout the stay at USI.

My sincere gratitude to my guide Mr Chudamani Ratnam for helping me shape this book in its present form.

My very special thanks to Dr Sangeeta Kaul who is a Network Manager at DELNET without whose timely assistance, writing this book would not have been possible.

I would also like to thank Lieutenant General P K Singh, PVSM, AVSM (Retired), Director, United service Institution of India, who motivated and encouraged me throughout the course of my fellowship.

Last but not the least , I must candidly accept that nothing would have been possible without the sustained support and constant help from my wife, Anita and my son Karan who always encouraged me to write this book.

India's Energy Security

Introduction

Energy Security is one of the most discussed, well deliberated and analysed areas in the strategic arena today. There has been a manifold increase in the energy consumption in the last few decades. It is attributed to the increasingly materialistic lifestyle, population growth, urbanisation, changing kinship structures, demographic transition and changing consumption patterns which needs increased production facilities and off course leads to higher consumption.

Energy plays the most pivotal role in the economic growth and security of any nation of the world. The future economic growth undoubtedly critically depends on the long term availability of the energy from the sources that are available, accessible and environment friendly. In recent times and over the turn of the century, energy has become an important factor in running economies. Due to the growth in demand, the competition for energy resources is becoming increasingly intense. This stiff competition is the concern and cause of "ENERGY SECURITY" of the nations as their economic independence depends on it.

India is facing a critical challenge of meeting a rapidly increasing demand for energy. India ranks fifth in the world in terms of total energy consumption. To meet the aspirations of 1.24 billion people of its population, it needs to identify the challenges facing the energy sector and frame policies to accelerate the development of the sector.

It has been indicated that if India wants to sustain 8 percent to 10 percent economic growth rate over next 25 to 30 years, If it is to eradicate poverty and meet its human development goals and to meet life line energy needs of all citizens by 2030. India needs to increase primary energy supplies by 3–4 times, electricity generation by 5 times, power generation capacity must increase to 8,00,000 MW from

1,60,000 MW. Also the requirement of coal needs to expand over 2 billion tons per annum by 2030. [1]

The uninterrupted energy supply is a vital issue for all countries especially for India at its present stage of development. The inadequate availability of energy resources could jeopardize not only India's economic progress but also security and strategic interests of the nation will be at stake. Hence adequate quantities of economically priced, clean sustainable and green fuel needs to be made available to the Indian consumers. Meeting the energy challenges is of fundamental importance to India's economic growth imperatives and its effort to raise the level of human development in the country which ranks low at 134 according to Human Development Index 2011 of the United Nations Development Programme. [2]

The other options available to India to address her energy security needs is by re–engineering its renewable and non-conventional sources like biomass, hydropower, wind energy, solar energy, geothermal energy, bio-gas, bio-fuel and hydrogen. Renewable energy technologies vary widely in their technological maturity and commercial status. In India, renewable energy is at the take–off point and a number of issues are to be addressed before these technologies could make a real difference in its better utilization which may lead to the economic development and safeguarding India's energy security concerns.

Definitions

The term ''Energy Security'' means different things for different people and to different countries. It is not feasible to define the entire scope through one single definition. An attempt is made here to reflect various definitions in order to cover the vastness of the concept of "Energy Security" from wider perceptions:

The Center for Global Partnership, Japan, defines energy security as maintaining necessary access to energy resources without risking the state's survival now and in future. [3]

Head of State Duma Committee for Electric Power, Transport and Communications Valery Yazev said that Energy Security means safeguarding the country against the threats of reliable fuel and power supply. [4]

The European Commission defines Energy Security IN ITS Green Paper 2000 as the ''uninterrupted physical availability of energy products on the market, at a price which is affordable for all consumers (private and industrial). [5]

Energy Security is a state in which consumers and governments believe, and have reasons to believe, that there are adequate reserves and production facilities available to meet their requirements in the near future. Or as a layman would understand it as it would be possible for him to buy and use energy in all forms at a reasonable cost at all times.(Canadian Energy Research Associate). [6]

From the above definitions, it is evident that the 'Energy security' is an umbrella term that covers many concerns and holistic views linking energy, economic growth and political power. It is not a stand-alone concept which can be defined in isolation as it is interdependent on many other aspects. The energy security perspective varies depending on one's position in the value chain. The consumers and energy intensive industries desire reasonably priced energy on demand and remains worried about disruptions in its supply. The major oil producing countries always consider security of revenue and of demand integral part of any energy security discussion while on the other hand Oil and gas companies consider access to new reserves, ability to develop new infrastructure, and stable investment regimes to be critical to ensuring energy security. On the contrary, the Developing countries are much concerned about the ability to pay for the resources to stimulate their economies and fear balance of payment shocks. The power companies are concerned with integrity of the entire network. The risks of supply disruptions and security of the infrastructure due to terrorism, war or natural disaster remains the concerns for the policy makers.

The traditional elements of energy security include supply sources, demand centers, geopolitics and market structure. [7]

References

1. Integrated Energy Policy : Report of the Expert Committee. New Delhi : Planning Commission, August 2006.

2. Human Development Index 2011. New York:United Nations Development Programme. (http://hdr.undp.org/en/statistics/hdl/)

3. www.cgp.org

4. Head of state Duma Committee for electric power, transport and communication.

5. http://ec.europa.eu/energy/green–paper–eng/

6. www.biee.org/wpcms/wp-content/

7. The New Energy Security Paradigm. World Economic Forum.

   http://members.weforum.org/pdf/ENERGY.PDF

Chapter –1

India's Energy Mix

Introduction

India with the estimated population of 1.24 billion is around 15 percent of the world's population and is the fifth largest consumer of energy resources. India's energy demand continues to rise drastically and exponentially, especially in the transport sector. India lacks sufficient energy resources and hence requires to import most of its energy resources in order to keep an equilibrium between the demand and the supply in the energy sector. In addition to pursuing domestic oil and gas exploration and production projects, India is also stepping up its natural gas imports, especially LNG (liquefied natural gas).

India's energy vulnerability is greater as could be seen in recent years. It has become an oil and natural gas importer which is likely to see an upsurge in future. It is very alarming and threatening trend which shows the dependency of the country on external sources for meeting the energy needs of the country and exposes the self–reliance of the country in the most important energy sector. Although current level of per capita energy consumption of India is extremely low as compared to rest of the world, with a moderate 8 percent growth of GDP, the energy mix size is projected to grow from 433.8 Mtoe in 2008 to 2123 Mtoe in 2030. [1]

India's concern over the energy security arises from increased dependence on overseas supply of oil and natural gas and coal. Overall, India's energy future appears to be dependent on high volume imports of fossil fuel materials.

According to International Energy Agency (IEA), coal accounts for nearly 40 percent of India's total energy consumption followed by nearly 27 percent for renewables and waste. Oil accounts for nearly 24 percent of total energy consumption, natural gas six percent, hydroelectric power almost two percent. Nuclear power comprises only one percent and other renewables less than 0.5 percent. [2] However it is likely to increase in light of civil nuclear energy cooperation deals with USA, France and other countries. In urban areas 93 percent had access to electricity compared to 50 percent in rural areas. Roughly 400 million people do not have access to electricity in India. [3]

Oil

According to Oil and Gas Journal, India has approximately 5.6 billion barrels of proven oil reserves which is over 0.5 percent of global reserves with total proven, possible reserves close to 11 billion barrels, the second largest in the Asia Pacific region. India produced roughly 880 thousand barrels per day in 2009 from over 3600 operating oil wells however it consumed 3 million bbl/d making it the fourth largest consumer of oil in the world. It is worth mentioning that 70 percent of oil was imported mostly from Middle East countries primarily from Saudi Arabia followed by Iran. EIA expects approximately 100 thousand bbl/d annual consumption growth through 2011. [4] India was the sixth largest net importer of oil in the world in 2009. EIA expects India to become fourth largest importer of oil by 2025 behind United States, China and Japan and that clearly indicates its growing dependency on the import of oil.

It has been reported that India is looking beyond the Gulf for seeking oil and to open up and explore new channels for the oil import. The investments in overseas oilfields by Indian Companies is expected to reach US $3 billion within a span of few years. India has also invested in Africa in Nigeria and Sudan. It has signed an agreement to purchase about 44 million barrels of crude oil per year on long term basis. India has invested in Syrian company for exploration and development of petroleum. [5] In recent years Indian oil companies have tried to acquire equity stakes in E&P overseas. ONGC Videsh Ltd (OVL) which conducts overseas operations in 13 countries including Sakhlain in Russia, Vietnam and Myanmar in South East Asia, Iran, Iraq, Sudan ,Brazil and Colombia. OVL's investment and its share in the Greater Nile Petroleum operating company (GNPOC) is 25 percent. OVL also holds 20 percent stake in Exxon–Mobil that operates Sakhlain 1 in Russia. Caspian basin is another area where India is trying to befriend the regions leaders and if possible gain a foothold. Also these revelations indicate the desperation and keenness of India to broaden its import capabilities as the demand is continuously increasing day by day. [6]

At the domestic front, the Indian government has drafted policies which are aimed at increasing exploration and production (E&P) of oil. As a part of an effort to attract oil majors with technical expertise, Ministry of Petroleum and Natural Gas created the New Exploration Licensing Policy (NELP) in year 2000. NELP VIII was launched in April 2009 and attracted $1. 1 billion investment. India is currently planning to launch NELP IX. This is a move towards creating an environment for self–sustainability. [7]

India has 2.8 million bbl/d oil refining capacity at 18 facilities. It has the fifth largest refinery capacity in the world. The major refineries are Reliance Industries, Jamnagar complex with refining capacity of 1.24 million bbl/d. It is the largest oil refinery in the World. Other upcoming projects are Vadinar refinery with 110,000 bbl/d, 120,000 bbl/d greenfield refinery in Bina,180,000bbl/d grassroots refinery in Bhatinda. [8]

Strategic Petroleum Reserves

To support India's energy security and a step towards its preparedness to encounter any eventualities in time of crisis, India is constructing a series of strategic petroleum reserves (SPR). The first storage facility at Vishakhapatnam, Andhra Pradesh will hold approximately 9.8 million bbl (1.33 million tons) of crude. The other facility at Mangalore, Karnataka will have a capacity of 11 million bbl (1.5 million tons). The third facility at Padur, Karnataka will have a capacity of 18.3 million bbl (2.5 million tons). The selection of coastal regions for storage facilities was made so that the reserves could be easily transported to refineries during the supply disruption. These facilities are expected to become operational soon. [9] In order to strengthen the energy security measures, availability of such Strategic Petroleum Reserves in large numbers all across the country needs to become operational.

Natural Gas

The natural gas is fast emerging preferred fuel of the future in view of it being an environmentally friendly and economically attractive fuel. According to OGJ India has approximately 38 trillion cubic feet (Tcf) of proven gas reserves. India's natural gas reserves comes from Bombay high complex on western off shores. The Bay of Bengal and Krishna–Godavari basin have added to India's energy security capabilities. Natural gas demand is expected to increase considerably owing to its large demand from power and fertilizer sector. It is worth reporting that the power and fertilizer sectors accounts for nearly three quarters of natural gas consumption in India. Despite the steady increase in India's natural gas production, demand has outgrown supply and India has been a net importer of natural gas. India's net imports reached an estimated 445 Bcf in 2009. [10]

The Gas Authority of India's (GAIL) current natural gas pipeline network extends approximately 4100 miles and its transmission capacity is approximately 5.2 Bcf /d.It plans to build close to 3800 additional miles of pipeline by 2013 with total transmission capacity being 10.6 Bcf/ d.

Natural Gas Imports

India's natural gas demand is expected to increase in coming years. To meet this growing demand, a number of import schemes including both LNG and pipeline projects have either been implemented or are being considered.

Liquefied Natural Gas

India began importing LNG in 2004. In 2008 India imported 372 Bcf of LNG nearly 75 percent from Qatar making it the sixth largest importer of LNG in the world. India has two operational LNG import terminals Dahej and Hazira terminals. Dahej terminal in Gujrat has a capacity of 5 million tons per year (mtpa) (975 Bcf/y). India's second terminal Hazira LNG has a capacity of 2.5 mtpa which could be expanded to 5 mtpa in future. The 5 mtpa LNG processing plant at Dabohl has now been commissioned. [11]

Cross Border Pipeline Projects

It is important to highlight the three main pipeline projects on which India is working currently. They are listed below: [12]

Iran– Pakistan–India Pipeline

IPI (Iran–Pakistan–India) pipeline has been under consideration since 1994 by Government of India. .The plan calls for nearly 1700–mile, 5.4–Bcf/d pipeline to run from South Pars fields in Iran to Gujarat in India. A large number of economic and political issues have delayed the project commencement. Indian government has made it clear that any import pipeline crossing Pakistan would need to be accompanied by a security guarantee from Islamabad.

Turkmenistan–Afghanistan–Pakistan–India Pipeline

India has also initiated its plans to work for the Trans Afghan Pipeline originating in Turkmenistan's Dauletabad natural gas fields and transporting the fuel to Afghanistan, Pakistan and India. TAPI is projected to have a capacity of 3.2 Bcf/d but work is yet to begin on the project. The major concern about the project is to ensure the security of the pipeline route, which would travel through the unstable, terror infected regions in Afghanistan and Pakistan and also it is not quite convincing whether Turkmen natural gas supplies are adequate to meet proposed export commitments.

India–Myanmar Pipeline Project

In order to strengthen the ties, India and Myanmar signed a natural gas supply contract in 2006. Initially the two countries had planned out to build a pipeline crossing the soil of Bangladesh. As the Government of Bangladesh was indecisive over the proposed plans to provide a sanction to the laying over of the pipeline from their region, both countries studied the possibility of building a pipeline that would terminate in state of Tripura in eastern India thereby not crossing Bangladesh soil. However, it is worth mentioning that In March 2009 Myanmar signed a natural gas deal with China sourced from a field invested in by GAIL and ONGC, putting the India–Myanmar deal in dilemma.

Other Proposed Projects

In order to secure supply of natural gas to India and meet the growing demands of the nation, India is currently looking to invest in liquefaction projects abroad. An example being, ONGC and UK based Hinduja Group are considering service contracts in Iran to supply 5 mtpa (975Bcf) of LNG to India. However industry analyst note that Indian companies appear unwilling to commit for long term LNG supply contracts at international prices. While negotiations are on for several long term deals, Whether India's bid will be accepted is questionable in light of the low prices that India has offered to pay. [13]

Electricity

India is generating a large amount of electricity to meet its growing needs. There is a tremendous widening of the gap between the demand and the supply.

In 2007, India had approximately 159 gigawatts (GW) of installed capacity and generated 761 billion kilowatt hours. Nearly all electric power in India is generated with coal, oil or gas. The conventional thermal sources produced over 80 percent electricity. The Hydroelectricity which is entirely a seasonally dependent source in India, accounted for 16 percent of power generated. Nuclear energy produced 2 percent of electricity while geothermal and other renewable sources accounted for 2 percent only.

In July 2010, India and Bangladesh signed a 35 years power import deal wherein India will import upto 500 megawatts beginning in 2012. India also imports electricity from Bhutan and Nepal. However these imports will not prove sufficient for lack of India's electric generation capacity. [14]

Electricity Shortages

India, the largest democracy of the world with an estimated population of 1.24 billion suffers from a severe shortage of electricity generation capacity. According to World Bank, approximately 40 percent residents in India are without electricity. Further worsening the situation is the total demand for electricity in the country which continues to rise dramatically and is completely outpacing the increases in the capacity. The chief reasons attributed for the low capacity building measures, have been the market regulations, insufficient investment in the sector and difficulty in obtaining environmental approval and funding. The Indian government is keen to bridge up the gap and to address this shortfall. The 11th plan set an ambitious target of adding nearly 79000

MW by 2012. Moreover the country also has electricity efficiency issues. In order to improve efficiency standards, Energy Conservation Act was passed in 2002 which has led to the establishment of Bureau of Energy Efficiency.

The Indian government also striving hard to focus on the development of nuclear power to meet its power generation targets. The Indo–US nuclear cooperation deal between the two countries is targeted to increase India's installed nuclear power generation capacity. Inspired by the collaborative deal, the government has set a target of 40000 MW by 2020. India currently has 14 nuclear reactors in commercial operations. India has recently bought six nuclear reactors from France and four from Russia. These ten nuclear reactors will add 11000 MW of electric capacity to the country which is much required by the nation. [15]

Hydropower and Other Renewables

In order to diversify the sources of electric power generation and increasing the country's capacity by the increased use of hydroelectric power, the Indian government has ambitious plans for undertaking new projects to tap the hydropower and other renewable resources for electric power generation in the country. The World Bank is also funding many of these projects. The statistics shows that the Geothermal, solar and wind power hold very little share in electric power generation in the country and a lot more needs to be done to bring them into the main stream resources. India is the only country to have a separate Ministry of New and Renewable Energy. [16]

References

1. Pode, Ramachandra. Addressing India's energy security and options for decreasing energy dependency. Renewable and Sustainable Energy Reviews. Vol 14(2010) pp 3017.

2. Energy Information Administration. Country Analysis Briefs : India. India Energy Data, Statistics and Analysis–Oil, Gas, Electricity, Coal (August 2010). www.eia.doe.gov

3. Ibid

4. Ibid

5. Pode, Ramachandra. Addressing India's energy security and options for decreasing energy dependency. Renewable and Sustainable Energy Reviews. Vol 14(2010) pp 3018.

6. Energy Information Administration. Country Analysis Briefs India. (August 2010). www.eia.doe.gov

7. Financial Express Newspaper. March 28, 2011.

8. Energy Information Administration. Country Analysis Briefs: India. (August 2010). www.eia.doe.gov

9. Ibid

10. Ibid

11. Ibid

12. Ibid

13. Ibid

14. Ibid

15. Ibid

16. Ibid

Chapter -2

Energy Security–Evolution and a Concept

Introduction

In the 21st century, the seamless, uninterrupted access to energy sources depend on a wide array of factors including the growing complex global markets, vast infrastructure network, the primary energy suppliers and its dependability on financial markets and technology. The Energy Security has been able to take a prominent position in the policy agenda of the governments around the world.

Energy Security–Evolution

The term energy security denotes unimpeded access or no planned interruptions to sources of energy, not relying on a limited number of energy sources, not being tied to a particular geographic region for energy sources, abundant energy resources, an energy supply which can withstand external shocks and /or some form of energy self-sufficiency. [1]

World War 1

Historically speaking, the genesis of using Oil instead of coal, goes back to the time of the World War I, when in April 1912 Winston Churchill made the decision to switch the fuel used by British Navy from Coal to Oil which proved a crucial edge over Germany. Though the oil supplies were from Iran rather than from Wales wherein coal supplies used to be made available, the company Anglo Iranian oil later became British Petroleum with huge investment from the British government and also an increased military presence in the Persian Gulf. Hence the notion that energy policy, foreign policy and national security are all interlinked is not new in nature. Since this war the concept of energy security has evolved and grown much complicated.

Energy Regime Post World War II

Usage of term energy security has evolved with change in the world's energy regime. This change signified dominance of non–renewable fossil fuels, liberalization of energy markets, the development of nuclear energy, growing demands of developing nations, impacts of political instability and large scale natural events.

Increasing Reliance on Oil

After World War II, Countries particularly those belonging to the Organization for Economic Cooperation and Development (OECD) became heavily dependent on Middle East oil as an energy source. This fossil fuel was an integral part of the post war economic growth and currently accounts for nearly 34% of world energy use (IEA 2009). The Oil was in abundance and cheap too until the oil price shocks of 1970's by the Organization of Petroleum Exporting Countries (OPEC) imposed restriction on the production. The shortfall in the global energy supplies led to formation of the International Energy Agency (IEA) with member countries required to hold oil stocks for sharing in an oil supply emergency. [2,3]

Liberalization of Energy Markets

By 1980s the global fraternity felt the need for greater competition and less government involvement and there has been a restructuring of markets subsequently. This entire process of restricting was encouraged by individual country governments and also by OECD, IMF and World Bank. [4]

Nuclear Energy

Following the Second World War, there was a sudden upsurge in using and producing nuclear energy for electricity generation. Twenty five countries including United States, United Kingdom, France, Germany and Russia had started generated electricity from the nuclear means. The two devastating accidents in 1979 and in 1986 (Three Mile Island in US and Chernobyl in former Soviet Union) significantly weakened the public acceptability for this source. [5] By the year 2008 nuclear energy accounted for 15% of world electricity generation compared to 41% by coal and 20% from gas.

Coal and Natural gas

Oil has become the main fuel for transport and replaced coal as industry's primary energy source with the development and expansion of oil pipelines and tanker infrastructures. The infrastructure development for natural gas has also led to availability of natural gas at lower prices and wider popularity of this particular primary energy source which accounts for almost a quarter of the world energy consumption. It is heartening to note that the consumption of natural gas has doubled since 1980 as infrastructure to overcome its transportation became increasingly available. The world's known natural gas reserves are as large as oil reserves but shipping constraints acted as bottlenecks for its development. These constraints have been removed with laying of pipelines across nations and the same is being transporting as liquefied natural gas (LNG). Natural gas resources are concentrated in handful of countries only. The former Soviet Union and Middle East hold 75% of known Natural Gas world reserves. [6]

Political instability and Extreme Natural Events

The entire process of energy import around the world is a very tricky and sensitive issue. The political instability in supplier countries can greatly affect and interrupt the supply chain process. The extreme events like 9/11 attacks in United States and extreme natural disasters like hurricane Katrina in 2005 and 2009 floods and bush fires in Australia also pose a major threats.

The Energy Regime of the 21st Century

As mentioned earlier, in the 21st century, the access to energy sources depends on open global markets and a vast infrastructure network of offshore platforms, pipelines, tankers, refineries, storage, generation capacity and transmission and distribution system. The cross border pipelines and strategic transport channels are highly important. The interdependence between industrialised countries and energy exporters have become much deepened, the financial markets and energy markets are linked up closely. This scenario depicts greater risk of major supply disruptions through political conflict of war, technical system failures, accidents, sabotage, extreme weather events or financial markets turmoil and looks to be entirely dependent on these factors. [7]

Energy Security–A concept

Energy security undoubtedly as demonstrated earlier is a multidimensional concept defined as reliable supplies at reasonable price. The secure supplies constitute the main factors including– supply security, sustainability and competitiveness. The Energy security or stability is all about security, any long interruption of a required flow of energy would immensely impact a nation's economic output, political stability and personal wellbeing of its citizens. The cross–sections of the society including private household, public authorities, business sector and government agencies are in dire need of energy to function; hence a regular supply of energy is a pre–condition for economic growth of a country.

The broader definition of energy security given by European Commissions green paper states that "energy supply security must be geared to ensuring the wellbeing of its citizens and the proper functioning of the economy the uninterrupted physical availability of energy products on the market, at a price affordable for all consumers while respecting environmental concerns and looking towards sustainable development" [8]

The other pertinent interlinked issues with Energy security which needs to be addressed are geopolitics of energy, links between energy and foreign policy, maritime safety of energy supplies and value of increased self–sufficiency.

In the Indian context if the 'security' in 'energy security' is considered as a protection from energy related threats then these threats can be categorised into two categories-those which affect economic growth and those which are unique to conditions of poverty. The threats which affect the economic growth –supply constraints, import dependency, costs are all energy and growth threats as they directly affect the economy of the country. Other threats like energy inequity, and use of traditional biomass fuels and their associated risks for the health can be taken as energy poverty threats. A new challenge which has emerged is a threat posed by climate change a large part of which is caused by fossil fuels, its consequences will pose development challenge to the developing world. From this it is evident that energy security and climate change are being regarded as competing objectives. India's 2006 Integrated Energy Policy Report defines energy security as follows. The country is energy secure when we can supply lifeline energy to all our citizens as well as meet their effective demand for safe and convenient energy to satisfy various needs at affordable costs at all times with a prescribed level considering hocks and disruptions that can be reasonably expected.

This definition caters for all aspects of energy security : especially those related to poverty and those aspects of energy security related to growth.

Multidimensional Aspects of Energy Security

It is in the fitness of things to discuss about the multidimensional aspects of Energy Security. ... SOURCE

The first inherent aspect of energy security is about management of risk–the risk of interrupted, unavailable energy supplies, risk of unaffordable energy prices, risk of insufficient capacities to meet demand, risk of relying on unsustainable sources of energy. These risks could be due to market instabilities, technical failure or physical security threats.

The second aspect concerns the extent to which energy security can reflect a country's energy use mix, abundance of local resources, and reliance on imports. The increased demand and projections of energy resources can be handled by bringing in various policy initiatives such as reducing demand, diversification of energy mix and supply source, investment in adequate capacity, emergency preparedness and improved energy access for business and citizens.

Thirdly, the term 'energy security' reflects a concept with strategic intent thereby implying that energy security is a concept and not a policy. Security of supplies consists of variety of approaches aimed at ensuring against supply risks. Security of supplies becomes a cost effective risk management strategy of governments, firms and consumers.

Fourth, the concept of energy security has a temporal dimension. The risk or threats to physical supply differs across short, medium and long term horizons. Short term risks include extreme weather conditions, accidents, terrorism attacks or technical failure. Long term risks concern the adequacy of supply to meet the demand and adequacy of infrastructure to deliver supply to markets. Therefore the meaning attributed to energy security will differ across time because the probability, likelihood and consequences of different risks or threats to supply will differ and vary over time.

Fifth aspect concerns the difference between energy markets. There are significant differences between the oil, gas, nuclear and electricity energy markets. Hence to apply the concept of energy security to the gas market will result in different meaning than if applied to the oil market or the electricity market and vice–versa.

References

1.   Chester, Lynne. Conceptualising energy security and making explicit its polysemic nature. Energy Policy, Vol 38(2010). pp 887–895.

2.   International Energy Agency (IEA) Key World Energy Statistics, 2008.

3.   Martin, W F, Harrje EM. The International Energy Agency. In Kalicki, JH, Goldwyn DL (Eds) Energy and Security : toward a new foreign policy strategy. Woodrow Wilson Press, Washington, pp 97–116.

4.   Chester, L. What are the outcomes and who benefits from the restructuring of the Australian electricity sector? (http://www.library.unsw.edu.au/~thesis/adt–NUN/public/adt–NUN20071017.113919) pp 16–26

5.   Thomas, S. Can nuclear power plants be built in Britain without public subsidies and guarantees ? Public Services International Research Unit, London : University of Greenwich, 2008.

6.   Yergin, D. Energy security and markets. In :Kalicki, JH, Goldwyn, DL (Eds) Energy and Security : towards a new foreign policy strategy. Woodrow Wilson Press, Washington, pp 51–64.

7.   Birol, F. Policy forum : the future of energy markets–world energy prospects and challenges. The Australian Economic Review, Vol 39(2), 2006, pp 190–195.

8.   European Commission Green Paper on Energy Security. http://ec.europa.eu/energy/green-paper-eng/

Chapter -3

India's Emerging Energy Challenges and Opportunities

India considered as a major economy of the world is growing rapidly and projected to become the third largest economy by 2020. Being the largest democracy, it is the country with largest section of poor population. Over 850 million Indians live below the poverty line with Rs 100 per day. 17% of the world population lives in India. India is the fifth largest consumer of fossil fuel with a share of 3.7 percent of global commercial supplies.

India's Energy Challenge

India's energy challenge can be best gauged from the fact that some 600 million Indians live without electricity and over 700 million still use biomass as the primary fuel for the most basic human need namely cooking .In majority of the rural India, biomass still remains as a most preferred and widely used fuel for cooking purposes. In the household sector more than 75% of the energy demand is for cooking purposes. India is rated very low in human development indices due to the lack of a proper and convenient availability of energy for the masses. Undoubtedly, India needs to maintain consistency in its GDP growth in order to bring a sea-change in the social and economic conditions of the people and must have an 8 percent GDP growth over next twenty five years to eradicate poverty and to meet its developmental goals. Providing access to modern commercial fuels at the affordable prices should remain the priority of the government. India is being pressurized by the global community to curb its fossil fuel consumption. Hence India needs to delink its economic growth from growth in energy consumption while ensuring access to lifeline levels of energy consumption. This is India's greatest energy challenge.

India's Energy Requirement and Challenges

In 2005–2006 India consumed about 513 million tons of oil equivalent (mtoe) of primary energy, 367 mtoe of commercial energy in which coal and lignite accounted for 38 percent , oil and gas accounted for 24 percent and 7 percent respectively, with hydro and nuclear contributing 2 percent and 1 percent of primary energy mix. [provide latest statistics]

According to the Integrated Energy Policy report 2006, India would sustain a growth of 8 percent till 2031–2032 and India's primary energy requirement would increase to about 1887 mtoe. This report estimated that the country's commercial energy requirement would increase more rapidly at the rate 5.2 to 6.1 percent over the 2005–2006 level, to the range of 1700 mtoe.

It was further reported in the above mentioned report that India's import dependence in 2005–2006 was about 24 percent of its total primary energy consumption and 33 percent of its commercial energy consumption in the same year. By 2031–2032 India's import dependence could rise to 49 percent of its primary consumption and 54 percent of the commercial energy consumption. [1] It is worth noting that India's incremental demand for commercial energy will rise to 21 percent of world's incremental supply of commercial energy. The gap between the demand and supply will threaten the economy of the nation

As stated above "the real issue is that India needs to grow her capabilities to be an emergent energy supplier and to grow her share of world production of fossil fuel. Thus the first threat and the challenge that India faces in meeting its energy needs is "availability or access to energy at an affordable price."

India has a strong technology in place for tapping Coal, which is 15 times more abundant than oil and gas, and therefore the second threat that India faces in meeting her energy needs is the ''pressure to reduce the country's incremental contribution to greenhouse gases." It also has a great impact on the pollution emission and the government is very sensitive on this issue. Even though India's per capita energy consumption in 2031-2032 is expected to be below that of China's consumption in 2005, about 16 percent of US consumption in 2005 and about 70 percent of world's average consumption in 2005. [2]

The third major threat to India's energy security is "lack of domestic energy infrastructure." India needs to grow its energy related infrastructure such as power generation ,transmission and distribution capacity, rail, road and port facilities as well as manufacturing, engineering and construction capacities to about eight fold times in next 25 years if energy supply and consumption targets are to be met.

Energy Alternatives and Energy Options

India has to gear up to embrace new energy alternatives and to have an out of box strategies to meet the growing energy needs of the country. Since no technological breakthrough is being forecast in developing new energy sources by 2031–2032 and India's growing energy demand is likely to account for a significant share of addition to the world fossil fuel supply, hence some of the key options for India to focus on in the future are as under

Energy Efficiency

The foremost important aspect in India's strategy for "efficient supply" remains energy efficiency and energy conservation. It has the great potential of reducing India's energy need by at least 20 percent. There is no other country in the world that has delivered an 8 percent + GDP growth over last five years with just a 3.7 percent growth in annual energy consumption. With 3.5 times the US population and 3 times the population of EU20, India has since 2002 delivered more than twice their growth while consuming lower amounts of fossil fuels. [3] It is praiseworthy to note that Indian industry has made stupendous efforts in achieving global energy efficiency standards in a number of energy intensive sectors. India has a strong potential and must bring into force the ways to improve energy efficiency in a number of sectors both on supply and demand side with particular emphasis on industry, buildings and transport. Energy efficiency and energy conservation are the most potent tools to ensure India's energy security as they can meet 20 percent of India's energy needs.

Clean Coal Technologies

We are aware that Coal, both domestic and imported is a key energy option for India. India must take lead in clean coal technologies (CCT), especially in situ coal gasification which can double the life of domestic coal from estimated 40-45 years based on conventional mining. The CCT programmes must be chalked out to strategically plan for the conceptualization, planning, development and commercial deployment of newer and more efficient coal utilization technologies in the country. It is to be noted that all of our current power plants are based on sub critical pulverized coal technology which needs up gradation and critical improvements .New technologies, such as super critical and ultra-super critical pulverized coal, Circulating Fluidized Bed Combustion (CFBC), and integrated gasification combined cycle (IGCC)technologies have much higher efficiencies than the current sub critical pulverized coal technology. However IGCC technology using Indian coal has not been successful but IGCC based on imported thermal coal is a major option for raising conversion efficiencies and reducing the carbon intensity of power generation. Similarly CFBC technology for the use of the low quality coal and lignite can also enhance India's energy options. [4]

Expand Hydrocarbon Supply Options

India doesn't have significant oil and gas resources and given the fact that oil and gas are likely to remain India's second largest energy source, India must exploit on shore deposits, especially in the northeast, seek for deep sea oil and gas and pursue alternate routes to hydrocarbons based on tar sands, shale gas ore emulsions ,methanol from gas fields and gas hydrates.

Energy diplomacy can help diversify both fuels and their sources of supply under long term arrangements thereby raising energy security. Such initiatives include transitional pipeline, equity oil and gas, equity coal and energy plantation in Latin America and Africa where some countries have advantage in production of bio-fuels.

Pursue an Informed Nuclear Policy

Expanding the use of nuclear energy for civilian use through international cooperation and speeding up the development of the domestic fast breeder technology to ultimately enable the use of domestic thorium remain national priorities that could deliver up to five percent of the energy mix by 2031-2032.

The nuclear option raises a debate encompassing social, economic and political dimension of sustaining energy and climate security. Disclosure and sharing of available knowledge in respect of uranium reserves and their likely civil nuclear power potential, risk of weapon proliferation and fissile material reaching wrong hands as a result of an expanded civil nuclear regime, the likely contribution of nuclear power in GHG abatement, public perception of safety, environmental and health concerns and economics of nuclear power including long term management of nuclear waste. While these five concerns are as real as the nuclear option itself, there is no justification for excluding nuclear or for that matter any other option that offers energy and climate security.

Market reforms and risk management

Most important element in all energy supply options is the existence of an efficient and competitive upstream and downstream energy markets with minimal price and tax distortions for both domestic and international players. It will create a political consensus around the fact that India's energy security would be boosted by roping a couple oil majors into the Indian markets. This would strengthen domestic energy markets and integrate them with global energy markets.

India also needs to prepare for energy supply disruption which is possible through strategic storage of oil and gas. Such storage of strategic oil and gas reserves can address the risk of technical and supply disruptions in addition to providing global price volatility

Technology acquisition

Acquisition of efficient commercial technologies that yield to higher efficiencies in energy, extraction, conversion, transportation, distribution, storage and end use can significantly increase India's ability to meet its future energy needs. National technology mission seek to expand India's domestic energy base through in situ coal gasification, clean coal technologies, bio-energy, solar energy, thorium and gas hydrates are all necessary for ensuring India's ability to meet its energy needs.

Implement an integrated renewable energy policy

The role of traditional fuels in India's energy mix cannot be overlooked when considering India's energy supply options. Traditional biomass will remain the third most important energy resource of India after coal and oil even in 2031–2032. It is projected to meet 10–12 percent of India's total primary energy consumption in 2031–2032.

Using India's land resource offers many energy alternatives and choices. The theoretical potential of bio energy is bigger by far than hydro, wind or nuclear. Under assumptions bio energy in India could potentially deliver some 2.5 times than the combined potential of all three together by 2031–2032. If it is assumed that India could actually find 60 million hectares of land for energy plantations, commercial wood plantation delivering the best known yields of 20 tons of wood per annum per hectare could meet 29–35 percent of India's primary energy requirements in2031–2032. However such bio energy potential can't be realized using only fallow or wasteland or non-arable land with intensive cultivation with water, fertilizer and pesticide.

To put this in perspective, 2.25 million hectares of land under solar cells with 15 percent conversion efficiency could yield the same energy as 60 million hectares of wood plantation and 7 to 8 million hectares of land under solar cells could give India total energy independence in 2031-2032. They do not need fertilizer or pesticide and use only water to clean collector surface.

As far as large scale hydroelectric power is concerned, exploiting the full hydro potential of 150,000 mw even though its contribution to energy mix remains two percent but still remains a high priority because of its ability to provide peak energy as well as water storage capacity. However hydropower has a number of environmental, governance and political hurdles to overcome apart from the issues of submergence,loss of forest land and biodiversity, there are many issues related to rehabilitation and sharing of waters that cause delay in realization of these projects.

Conclusion

India's ability to deliver an annualized growth of eight percent + over the next 25 years is critically dependent on its ability to reliably secure and supply the modest levels of energy required for this growth. Making this growth inclusive and ensuring all round development in human development parameters requires that India delivers lifeline levels of modern, commercial energy to all its citizens. This is a huge challenge which is fraught with threats, such as availability at affordable prices environmental constraints and non-availability of energy infrastructure. Efficient and sustainable use of energy will make this challenge more manageable and increase India's ability to deal with potential threats.

References

1. Sethi, Surya. India's energy challenges and choices.In Noronha, Ligia and AnantSudarshan (eds). India's Energy Security. London :Routledge, 2009. pp 19-28.

2. Integrated Energy Policy Report 2006. New Delhi ; Planning Commission, 2006

3. World energy assessment (UNDP) energy and challenge of sustainability.

4. Chikkatur, Ananth P. Making the best use of India's coal resources. Economic & Political Weekly, Vol 40(52), December 2005, pp. 5457–5461.

Chapter –4

Energy and Poverty at house–hold level in India

Introduction

Poverty has a multidimensional notion. It relates to number of inter related deprivations–lack of access to adequate income, food, water, clothing, shelter, sanitation, healthcare and education. Although poverty does not directly include energy as a component but at the most fundamental level energy delivers cooked food, water, health and education services.

Energy poverty has been defined as the absence of sufficient means of accessing adequate, affordable, reliable, high quality, and environmentally safe services to support human development. [1,2] People who are considered 'energy poor' often rely heavily on traditional biomass fuel for cooking and lack access to even minimum electric lighting.

India alone accounts for 50 percent of energy–impoverished people who are highly dependent on traditional cooking fuels, and for 40 percent of people without access to modern electricity. [3,4] The dependence on biomass causes more than 400,000 premature deaths (mostly women and children) in India annually.

Cooking fuel is severely inadequate in rural areas. Firewood is still the most sought after fuel in the rural sector. Many rural poor are also dependent on purchased firewood as a result of firewood's decreasing availability. This trend is more common in rural rich and urban poor and use of electricity is associated with people who are well off in India.

The disparities and inequalities in access to modern energy are growing between urban and rural households, between different geographical regions and people with various income groups. While access to electricity and LPG is increasing in both urban and rural sector, the rate of penetration is very slow in rural sector due to low purchasing power and poor availability of these fuels in remote rural areas.

Energy Poverty Problem

"Energy poor" or energy vulnerable people have limited livelihood opportunities, lack of basic education, lack of regular cash flow and other social services. Their lesser ability to pay for modern fuels and energy using equipment results in use of inefficient traditional fuels. Improved energy though available, is often not easily accessible in remote areas. It is financially unviable for a state to have a distribution network to meet the energy demands of widely scattered low energy consuming communities. [5] Consequently the poor find themselves using traditional dirty fuels (firewood, cow dung and crop residues) and inefficient devices that provide little useful energy. In turn they expose themselves (especially women and children) to indoor pollution resulting from combustion of solid fuels. In addition to severe cost of health and time, being unable to use modern energy and equipment results in lower productivity and poor quality output and thus consequently, lower incomes from economic activities such as agriculture farming. This leads to lower returns for labour and invested capital, resulting in smaller surplus for reinvestment, resulting in so called 'energy poverty trap'. [6]

As a result of increased deforestation, there is growing commercialization of firewood even in rural India resulting in many poor people paying cash for firewood and highly priced electricity thereby spending larger portion of their low income on fuel and light. A Number of studies in India and developing countries have shown that fuel choices depend on various factors where monetary cost, ease of availability, gender issues, may all combine to encourage the use of traditional biomass fuels over more efficient modern alternatives. They do adapt to modern fuels like LPG but continue using fuel wood. Irregularities in supply of modern fuels like LPG, high initial cost and maintenance cost are prime factors that hinder the complete and smooth shift towards the use of modern fuels from traditional ones. [7,8]

The 'Energy Poor' are placed at a distinct disadvantage compared to rest of the population .The poor consume significantly less energy and use different and traditional technologies as compared to well off. For instance, the poor with limited access and affordability use minimum electricity for lighting and are generally unable to take advantage of modern facilities available to others (such as electricity based agricultural production) that are necessary to break the vicious cycle of poverty.

Patterns of Household Energy Use In India

Patterns of Energy Use for Cooking

The major cooking fuels in India are firewood and chips, dung cakes and LPG According to a survey 60.5 percent households use firewood and chips as primary source of energy for cooking, about 7 percent use dung, 3.5 percent used kerosene and 22 percent used LPG.

In rural India, household primarily uses three sources of energy for cooking–firewood and chips, dung cakes, and LPG. It is also seen that a constant percentage (75–78%) of rural household are dependent on firewood and chips ,due to their cheapness and easy availability, 46 percent of households obtain them through free collection about 21 percent depend on home grown stock, and 23.7 percent make cash purchases. Whereas the use of LPG has gradually increased in rural India from 1.9 percent in 1993–94 to 12.6 percent in 2010–11 owing to its improved availability however the use of dung cakes has declined only marginally from 11.5 percent in 1993–94 to 7.1 percent in 2010–11, which is a cause of concern.

In urban India, LPG is the most commonly used primary cooking fuel, followed by firewood and chips, and kerosene. More and more households have shifted from firewood and kerosene to LPG. In 2009–10 67.1 percent of urban household used LPG as their primary cooking fuel as compared to just 29.5 percent in 1993–94. LPG may have displaced kerosene more than it has displaced firewood the decline in the use of kerosene from 23.2 percent to 10.2 percent is greater than the decline in the firewood and chips from 30percent to 21.7 percent. Firewood is the second most commonly used primary cooking fuel. With more than one–fifth of population dependent on it as a primary source of cooking energy. Unlike rural India it is a commercialized fuel in urban India with about two third of urban households having purchased the fuel. [9]

Household energy use is also based on occupation groups of the householders–defined as agriculture labour, non–agriculture labour, self–employed in agriculture, other households having diversified income sources, regular wage earners or casual labours etc. Agricultural labourers usually live in very poor conditions, have low opportunity costs of time, and thus largely depend on freely available fuels. In the urban sector, the use of solid fuels was highest among casual labourers and lowest among regular wage earners. Higher wages in the urban sector make it economically sensible for households to switch to more efficient fuels and appliances.

In rural areas, the scheduled tribes (90%) and schedule castes (77.2%) use larger amounts of traditional fuels as compared to other classes. Although these social groups usually live in poor and backward areas, this may also suggest the existence of access discrimination (like rationed kerosene). In urban sector, LPG is the most commonly used fuel across all social groups.

Statistics show significant geographical variation in patterns of use in rural India. LPG has highest penetration in three states with high income, Punjab (24 percent), Haryana (19 percent), and Kerala (18 percent). Similarly in the urban sector, Punjab (70 percent), Haryana (72.9 percent) and Gujarat (62.3) percent are the highest users of LPG. Poorer states largely have a lower penetration of modern fuels (such as Bihar, Orissa, Chhattisgarh, Assam and Jharkhand). One also observes an absence of relationship between a state's income and the fuel mix, for example Kerala (urban), one of the most developed states, is observed to have much higher dependence on firewood and chips (48.4 percent) and a corresponding low LPG penetration (43.7 percent) as compared to Assam (urban : 27.2 percent firewood and chips and 60.6 percent LPG) and Rajasthan (urban : 38.6 percent firewood and chips and 51.3 LPG). This is reflective of the fact that Kerala is a heavily forested state where wood is readily available. Similarly in high income rural Punjab, where dairy farming is wide spread, a large number of households (33.3 percent) use dung as a primary cooking fuel. Thus easy availability is an important determinant of traditional fuel use.

Patterns of Energy Use for Lighting

In India, kerosene and electricity are two major sources of energy accounting for 99 percent of households in both urban rural India. Over a period of time electricity is replacing kerosene as a source of lighting both in rural and urban India. Between 1993–94 and 2009–10 about 25 percent of households in rural India shifted from kerosene to electricity as against 12 percent in case of urban India.

Many households with access to electricity exhibit significant consumption of kerosene for lighting, particularly in rural sector .this shows that these houses may be using kerosene based lamps in case of electricity failure also households connected to electricity have not necessarily made the transition away from kerosene completely as it is being used as a backup fuel in case of electricity failure.

70 percent of households in low income group in rural areas depend on kerosene to meet their primary lighting requirement. This can be explained by high installation cost of electricity services and equipment, poor quality housing, mobile lighting which is better achieved by kerosene. In urban India on the other hand access to electricity depends not on income as the majority of household use electricity in all income groups. In urban India the difference in electricity access between the richest and poorest appears to be less as compared tom rural sector.

In rural India access to electricity is found to be least among the agriculture labourers (47.6percent) however in urban India use of electricity is highest amongst regular salary earners (97 percent) and lowest among casual labourers.

There is a significant geographical difference in electrification. The use of electricity is found to be positively correlated with level of income in different states. In rural India, use of electricity was highest in Punjab (96 percent) followed by Haryana (90 percent) Karnataka (86 percent) Tamil Nadu (84.6 percent) and Andhra Pradesh (84 percent). The proportion of household using electricity is lowest in Bihar (10 percent), Uttar Pradesh (24 percent) Jharkhand (26 percent), Assam (30 percent), and Orissa (31.5 percent), There are also states with greatest number of villages not connected to electricity. Apart from Punjab, Haryana and two middle income states of Andhra Pradesh and Maharashtra (with large net sown area and large irrigated land) have high rural electrification because electricity is used in agricultural pumping and cropping. In urban India, in 10 out 17 major states over 90 percent of households obtain their lighting requirements from electricity. In urban areas the percentage of households using electricity is again found to be lowest among two poorest states–Bihar (68 percent) and Orissa (70 percent). [9]

Major Constraints In Transition to Modern Fuels

The current growing trends in energy use clearly show that neither growth in income nor the affordability of alternatives can alone bring about change to use modern fuels. There are numerous other factors, such as fuel availability, culture, geography, the extent of urbanization, fuel prices, and state policies that influence the fuel choice.

Also the reason that traditional fuels have persisted is that the Indian Government has been unable to provide affordable, abundant, and highly reliable modern alternatives. The energy policies tend to have an urban bias with much focus on commercial fuels–coal oil and gas–catering for urban energy consumption and growth. [10] Some of the major problems in this context are discussed below.

Poor Targeting of Subsidies and Programmes

Subsidies in the past have been largely mis targeted. LPG subsidies tend to benefit the people who are well off much more than truly poor because of the greater consumption and greater ease of access those who are wealthier A World Bank study suggested that three quarter of the subsidy went to the urban households, four fifth of which was given to the top 50 percent of the population (UNDP).

In case of kerosene, a significant fraction of the subsidized fuel is illegally used to adulterate diesel. The remaining kerosene that does reach consumers suffer from poor targeting as for LPG subsidies. (UNDP)

Most of the electrification programmes focus more on the number of villages connected to electricity than households. Some of the schemes meant for people below poverty line have not been successful due to large scale leakage and flat rates regardless of level of consumption.

Subsidies have meant that LPG supplies are limited and electricity supply, even where grid connections are available, is highly unreliable. Similarly while kerosene has many advantages over fuels such as firewood, it too needs to be subsidized. Extending energy resources to vast rural population will necessitate large increase in the Imports of the fossil fuels. With the need to find long term credible solutions to concerns about the country's energy security, chances of complete elimination of traditional fuels in foreseeable future are very small. The use of traditional fuels is not undesirable in itself – it is the manner in which they are used is a problem. To understand why rural policies have not succeeded as well as India would like it .it is essential to understand and appreciate the complexities of energy poverty problems.

Clean fuels tend to be losing out due to the cost factor. A large number of rural household are characterized by low purchasing power as well as access to fuels such as dung, crop residue or wood at no monetary cost and using them to cook is a serious health hazard. However bulk of this is borne by women and children who possess less negotiating power in the household. Decision to spend money on bio-gas plants or LPG with new gas chullahs are strongly influenced by men. Within the household the value of the women's time is regarded as very low and with the brunt of the health costs not being borne by the person making purchasing decisions and these are not factored in while making energy choices. Consequently it becomes harder to convince many rural households of the value of paying for either clean technologies, or cleaner fuel such as LPG. [10]

Policy Implications

The most important question for policy makers is how to guide fuel switching process along a sustainable pathway and how to ensure that it occurs as smoothly as possible. Some of the issues that need to be kept in mind when framing policy with the objective of encouraging households to shift to newer and better forms of energy are as appended in succeeding paragraphs.

Addressing Energy Affordability

As poor households have low income and they spend a significant proportion of their income on fuels for cooking and lighting the issue of energy affordability becomes important. The smart LPG and kerosene subsidies specifically directed towards poor and financial support for initial capital and non–recurrent cost can go a long way towards enabling poor households to make more efficient choices. [11]

Enabling Widespread Access

It has been seen that affordability alone is not enough to motivate shifts in energy use. Enabling widespread access to modern alternatives is also crucial for transitions to work. Unfortunately when fuel supply and distribution system are controlled by state (such as for kerosene and LPG in India), there tends to be inequities in distribution (with major urban areas being far better served than more remote and widely scattered locations), black markets and corruption. Hence unless and until easy access to modern fuel is made available, equitable and widespread use is unlikely to be seen.

As far as electricity is concerned a similar problem occurs if low ampere connections are not available. In many cases rural consumers do not require connections rated for higher loads, since they are not looking to run many appliances that might be used in high income urban setting. Thus ensuring the availability of electrical connections that takes into account the needs of the consumer is important. [10]

Taking Cognizance of Gender Realities

Energy poverty is linked quite closely with gender roles and the earning power and empowerment of woman. Energy policy must be framed with fact in mind. It is essential to convince of them of the utility of the new technologies such as solar cookers and cooking stoves. Since it is often men who are decision makers when it comes to spending money on the new technology it is important that both men and women are be a part of technology dissemination process. [10]

Decentralization, Modern Renewables and Sustainable Biomass

Decentralized electricity generation, especially through the use of modern renewable solar photovoltaic and sustainable use of biomass, provides options that should be at the forefront of developing country like India. They have an invaluable role to play in in providing lifeline amounts of clean energy especially in remote areas where grid electrification is difficult. With optimistic projections technologies such as wood gasifiers biogas plants and spread of farm forestry and natural forest management can make a huge difference towards reducing energy inequities and improving energy access. [10]

References

1. Barnett, A. Energy and the fight against poverty. Livelihood sector report, UK : Department for International Development, 2000. www.livelihoods.org/post/ Docs/ABISSI3a.doc

2. Reddy, AKN. Energy and social issues. In World Energy Assessment. New York : UNDP, 2000.

3. China and India insights. World Energy Outlook. Paris : IEA, 2007.

4. Human Development Report 2007–2008. New York : Palgrave Macmillan, 2007.

5. Ramani, K V and Heijindermans, E. Energy, poverty and gender : a synthesis. Washington, DC : The World Bank, 2003.

6. Smith, K R and Mehta, S. The burden of disease from indoor air pollution in developing countries : comparison of estimates. Paper prepared for US Agency for International Development and World Health Organization, 2000.

7. Ramani, K V and Heijindermans, E. Energy, poverty and gender : a synthesis. Washington, DC : The World Bank, 2003.

8. Heltberg, R. Fuel switching : evidence from eight Developing countries. Energy Economics, Vol 26(5), 2004. pp 869–887.

9. Gupta, Eshita and AnantSudarshan. Energy and poverty in India. In Noronha, Ligia and AnantSudarshan. India's Energy Security. London : Routledge, 2009. pp 34–43

10. Ibid

11. Heltberg, R. Fuel switching : evidence from eight Developing countries. Energy Economics, Vol 26(5), 2004. pp 869–887.

Chapter –5

Role of West Asia and Central Asia in India's Energy Security

Energy Security

Energy security is a must for every country today. Economic growth rates and development are directly related to the assured access each country has to energy resources. So is the case with India. Talmiz Ahmed described energy security as "an assured access to energy resources, at affordable prices to obtain sustainable economic growth rates and economic development."

He adds: "Most of the world energy comes from hydrocarbons (oil & gas), which account for 65% of world's energy requirements. While oil accounts for 42% of global energy mix, the other sources of global energy are coal (24%), natural gas (22%), nuclear energy (6%) and renewable and non–conventional sources (7%). World energy demand has increased by 95%over the last 30 years and is expected to rise by 60% over the next 20 years. During this period the demand for oil will increase by 42% while the demand for gas will increase by 97 %." [1].

Table 5.1 Global Oil Demand Forecast : 2025 (in million tons per year)

	2001	2025
Asia: Big 4 (China, Japan, ROK and India)	946.2	1842.6
Rest of Asia	298.8	547.8
Middle East	249	448.2
North America	1195.2	1743
West Europe	697.2	697.2
Rest of the World	448.2	647.4
Total	**3834.6**	**5926.2**

From the above table we notice that there is a shift in the consumption pattern of Asia–produced hydrocarbon fuels from Western Europe and North America to Asia. 95% of Asian gas and 55% of Asian crude is now being consumed in Asia.

Global Energy Scenario in West Asia and Central Asia

West Asia

The global reserves of oil are not uniformly distributed. 65% of the resources are located in the gulf in Iran, Iraq, Kuwait, Saudi Arabia and UAE. Their reserves comprise 92 billion tons of oil and 1110.5 million tons of oil are produced annually with 90% capacity to produce excess oil as per global standards. [3]

The expansion of production capacity can be enhanced by the Gulf OPEC producers at a cost that is relatively small percentage of projected gross revenues. According to the International Energy Agency (IEA), the Gulf region's oil production capacity, between 2006 and 2030, would expand from 27 MBD to 45 MBD (1,344 to 2,241 million tons per year). The region would then represent 40% of the world's oil supply, and would account for three fourths of additional global supply from 2006 to 2030. [4]

According to the estimates made Asia holds major resources of gas. The Asian part of Russia has 27% of world's proven reserves, followed by Iran (15%) and Qatar (14%). Thus major gas reserves are held by North and Central Asia and the Gulf countries. [5]

Central Asia and Caspian Sea Region

The Caspian region, mainly the area around the Caspian Sea is rich in oil resources. As per EIA data, the total proven oil reserves in Caspian Sea region range from 2,320 to 6,683 million tons and total proven natural gas reserves are estimated at 6,496 billion cubic meters (EIA 2007). This reveals that 4% of total oil reserves of the world and five percent of total gas reserves are in this region. [6]

From the details of the Gulf and Central Asian gas reserves given along with other reserves we notice that there is more focus on Central Asian hydrocarbons resources. It is important to consider that there are limitations in terms of quantity and accessibility to Central Asian reserves. It may be noted that the Caspian area has emerged as an important alternative source of oil and gas supply.

Table 5.2 Global Gas Reserves (in trillion cubic meters)

Region	tcm
Russia/Central Asia	53.2
West Asia	56
Africa	11.2
South &South East Asia	8.4
North America	5.6
South /Central America	5.6
Europe	4.2
Australia	2.8

India's Energy Scenario

Hydrocarbon vision 2025, published by Government of India in Feb 2000 (GOI 2001), [7] gives a bleak view of India's energy security predicament: its crude oils self–sufficiency had declined from 63% in 1989–90 to 30 percent in 2000–2001. The situation is likely to get worse and is equally grim in case of natural gas.

The Integrated Energy Policy document published by Planning Commission in August 2006 takes a holistic view of India's energy requirements needed to meet a minimum growth rate of 8% per annum until 2031–2032 i.e the end of 15th Five Year Plan. [8]

According to it there is a high level of dependence on imports and also there is the need to obtain internationally developed technologies to enhance the country's domestic resources and capabilities, India has committed itself to pursuing a robust 'Energy Diplomacy' this consists of substantial, pro–active and multifaceted engagements across the world to promote India's energy security interests. The overseas engagements are aimed at achieving the following:-

• "Significant enhancement of domestic resources and

capabilities by bringing in the state–of–the–art foreign technologies and expanding the national knowledge base.

• Acquisition of assets abroad, involving either equity participation in producing fields; and/or exploration and production (E&P) contracts in different parts of the world both onshore and offshore.

• Participation in downstream projects (refineries and petrochemicals) in producer and consumer countries on the basis of criss–cross investments.

• Setting up of transitional gas pipelines.

• Obtaining technologies to promote sustainable energy use, including conservation, increased–friendly fuels."

India's Perception of Energy Security

Over the period India has realised its dependency on external oil resources which are predominantly in the Gulf and central Asian regions. India can not ignore the relevance of these countries to its energy security interests. The Gulf and Central Asia have thus a crucial place in the pursuit of India's energy security interests. Globally, these regions attract considerable international attention and thus both these regions are politically volatile. This volatile situation disturbs the internal situation in the countries as external forces are competing in this region for power and influence. India has not been acting as a disturbing factor but as a partner by setting up alliances in Gulf and Central Asia. Joint proposals that emerge out of this cooperation help the countries. These proposals cover the hydrocarbon value chain and includes prospecting in each other's territories, and exchanges in regard to R & D technology, safety norms and training. Bilateral relations are important and also enable Indian and foreign companies to work together on specific projects in third world countries. [9]

India's Energy Diplomacy in Gulf and Central Asia

The two-thirds of India's oil requirements are fulfilled by the Gulf region. Saudi Arabia, among these countries is India's largest supplier of crude oil, meeting 25% of its annual requirements. As a follow up of the visit of King Abdullah bin Abdul Aziz in January 2006, the two countries agreed to transform their commercial ties into a 'strategic energy partnership. This, it was agreed to be done through investments in each other's petrochemical projects, and also through India's participation in Saudi Arabia's upcoming proposal in Gas Sectors. Besides Saudi Arabia, Iran is India's other major energy partner in the Gulf; It is the third largest supplier of oil to India (at 2.5 MT/y, after Saudi Arabia and Nigeria) and it is emerging as an associate in a number of hydrocarbon related projects particularly in gas sector. The other major partners of India include the UAE, Kuwait and Oman. Qatar has emerged as an important source of gas.

In order to further strengthen its energy security, India has also turned its attention to Central Asia and Turkey. In Kazakhstan Indian companies are pursuing E&P proposal in the Caspian. The possibility of purchasing Azeri oil at Ceyhan was also examined; this led to the first shipment of central Asian oil to India in 2005. [10]

India and the Gulf

From the efforts India has been making, it is observed that India has enduring interests in Gulf and Arab Peninsula. The region has emerged as India's Security Perimeter and any developments in the region have a direct bearing on India's security and strategic interests. While Gulf and Arab Peninsula contribute a great deal to India's crude oil requirements, providing over two thirds of annual imports, security of these oil facilities remain to be of India's major long term interest

India's political and economic strengths based on its democratic and multicultural character its high growth rates and its firm technological base, all of which have helped ince the late 1990s convince the GCC countries that India was poised to play an enhanced regional and even International role in economic and technological arena. These perceptions led the GCC foreign ministers to invite India as a dialogue partner, only the fourth after USA, EU and Japan. The first GCC-India industrial conference as a result, was held in Feb 2004, when six Commerce and Industry Ministers from GCC countries and Indian minister for commerce and Industry came out with the 'Mumbai Declaration' to enhance economic cooperation by focusing on four select priority areas; trade; Investments; Industrial Cooperation; and transfer of technology including information technology. [11]

India and Central Asia

Since the emergence of Karzai–led government in Kabul, India's focus on Central Asia has shifted from security to business. India's total bilateral trade with the region is about US$300 million per annum, primarily dominated by the trade ties with Kazakhstan. In spite of considerable effort over the last few years, presence in the Central Asia energy sector remains modest. It is limited to a 15% holding by ONGC Videsh Limited in Kazakhstan's Alibekmola oil field and a 10% holding in country's Kurmangazi oil field. Gas Authority of India Limited (GAIL) was awarded two fields for exploration of gas in Uzbekistan in April 2008.

Besides commercial interests in Central Asia, India has political and strategic interests, centered round the objective that the area remain peaceful and progressing. It does not want extremist forces like the Taliban to destabilize the region. The Central Asian countries support this ideology. This ideology has contributed to the expanding political and economic ties between India and the other countries in Central Asia. With Iran, there has been a regular exchange of visits between Indian and Iranian leaders. India has been vigorously pursuing the Iran–Pakistan–India gas pipeline project over the last few years in spite of sustained US Public criticism of the project. This project could possibly include Russia and China as active participants' .Senior Russian and Chinese officials and corporate heads have repeatedly indicated the interests of their companies in participating in the project. [12] According to Liu Xeucheng, director of the Beijing Centre for American studies and a senior fellow of China Institute for international studies

"The US is trying to coordinate with all countries around Iran in order to isolate it—— India and China have good relations with US but must follow their own strategy on Iran. If India gives up on Iran in the hope for securing nuclear energy from the US, it may end up with nothing. India will lose its strategic pipeline and US might also abandon the nuclear deal at some point in future. Pipelines from Central Asia are a strategic lifeline for India's energy security." [13]

India's Multilateral Engagement and Strategies

In order to follow its policy of promoting peace and economic development in Central Asia and the other neighbouring, India has been engaging itself at multilateral level on a number of platforms. First among these is Shanghai Cooperation Organization (SCO), where India has observer status. The SCO clearly provides a valuable institutionalized arrangement for Russia and China to ensure that their interests, in a region of considerable strategic and economic importance to them are not abridged by expanding American Influence. On their part, the Central Asian countries too, see the Russian and Chinese presence as providing a valuable counterweight to the American influence, thus guaranteeing them much more autonomy. [14]

India has been attaching greater importance to gas-pipeline from Central Asia and seeking cooperation from the countries concerned. India has been conscious of the fact that Turkmenistan–Afghanistan–Pakistan–India (TAPI) is an important project not only in terms of meeting Pakistani and India's energy needs but also it would provide Afghanistan with transit fees and possibly even the chance to develop Afghanistan's own gas reserves. The project has considerable geopolitical significance in that, for the first time South Asia would have access to gas from Central Asia. Once the pipeline is operational, it is possible that Turkmenistan could evolve from a single source of gas to the pipeline into a regional hub, with pipelines from neighbouring countries such as Uzbekistan, Kazakhstan, Azerbaijan, and even Russia, linking up with the pipeline to meet the increasing demand of South Asia. This arrangement would contribute to having a pipeline from Caspian region that could also go to LNG terminals on the Gulf to transport Central Asian LNG to South East Asia and North East Asia.

Iran has the world's largest gas reserves. As such the 1900 k.m. long Iran–Pakistan–India (IPI) gas pipeline project would have a sound commercial base. But the pipeline from the Iranian collection center of Assaluyeh on the Gulf to the Indian borders would be well within the range of economical gas supply by pipeline vis–a–vis LNG. But the main issue is that the IPI project is not a trilateral government–to–government project; it would be owned by an international consortium made up of national companies of three countries. The ownership of the project by an international consortium and the fact that Pakistan itself would be a major consumer of the gas would severely limit Pakistan's ability to tamper with the pipeline.

India considered that there was a need to have the Asian-Producer-Consumer Dialogue to streamline issues concerning the purchase of oil and gas by India. India convened a Round Table of Asian Oil Ministers in Delhi in January 2005. It was observed during the conference that Asian Producers and Consumers would obtain stability, security and sustainability through mutual interdependence, which called for mutual investments in each other's countries. The ministers of all the countries envisaged a future 'in which Asian countries can become major participants in the massive investment which needs to be made in the Asian countries represented at the table, running to an estimated 1,580 billion dollars over next 25 years in upstream, midstream and downstream Oil and Gas development in all the countries put together. [15]

A Second Round Table conference was held in Delhi in November 2005 where the ministers of consumer countries met ministers from North Asia (Russia) and Central Asia. The assembled dignitaries agreed to study 'the promotion of developing gas and oil interconnections through LNG and through transitional oil and gas pipelines within the Asian region for integration of energy markets as well as improving the transportation infrastructure.

In the 2011 Round Table conference of 18 Asian countries, including India and 3 international organizations it was observed that oil and gas supply needed to meet future global requirements. However, it was agreed to limit excessive oil price volatility and initiated Joint Organizations Data Initiative (JODI) as a means to enhance market data transparency. They agreed to increase energy efficiency measures to be introduced in developing countries.

In order to facilitate the flow of oil and gas, there was a need to establish the network of pipelines towards the East and South. It was noted that thousands of kilo meters from Russia, Central Asia and North Sea to Western Europe, hardly any pipeline move eastwards and southwards. The Asian Gas Grid envisages the setting up of series of pipelines that will carry natural gas from North and Central Asia and the Gulf to various consumption centres in South and East Asia. Some of the proposed pipelines in the proposed grid are Russia–Kazakhstan–Iran pipeline to the Gulf, Myanmar–China pipeline, the Sakhalin–Nakhodka–ROK–China pipeline, Uzbekistan–Turkmenistan–Azerbaijan pipeline, Iran–Pakistan–India pipeline, Turkmenistan–Afghanistan–Pakistan–India pipeline. According to the current estimates, additional pipelines required to realize the Asian Gas Grid would be about 22,500 km, costing about $ 22 billion. [16]

Viability of Central Asian Energy Resources

The Central Asian countries are landlocked. Yet India's efforts to circumvent the barriers that exist in the flow of gas and oil to India through these countries remain a major issue of concern. The region poses several problems as compared to the Gulf. Central Asia lacks the technical infrastructure required to ensure rapid petroleum development. The operation is expensive as compared to the Gulf. If the Central Asian Gas was to be sent to South Asia and East Asia through pipelines, it would be fairly expensive.

The uncertain legal status of the Caspian Sea is also hindering the further oil and gas exploration and development in the area. The five littoral states have not been able to agree on a plan to divide the sea's resources, including the oil rich sea bed. Azerbaijan, together with Russia and Kazakhstan, have advocated establishment of a maritime boundaries based on equidistant division of the sea, but Iran and Turkmenistan disagree. The Caspian Sea has six separate hydrocarbon basins, although most of its oil and gas resources have not been developed as yet. [17]

The security of the pipelines is a major issue and India's concerns pertaining to the viability of transitional pipelines. The major concern is the possibility of attacks on pipelines passing through the disturbed province of Baluchistan in Pakistan. Yet another issue is the uncertain and deteriorating bilateral relations between India and Pakistan and that the Pakistani Government could stop and deny India the gas needed for its power and industrial projects. Similarly with regards to a proposed pipeline project to India from Turkmenistan, via Afghanistan and Pakistan there are doubts whether Turkmenistan has the gas reserve to justify the pipeline and whether the uncertain situation in Afghanistan also inhibits progress on the project. However, good bilateral relations are a must for initiating discussions on pipeline projects and each country has to be dependent on the gas and oil coming through the pipelines. This is not happening.

Conclusion

India's broad based constructive energy related engagement with West Asia and Central Asia are important. There is a need to supplement these efforts with each country through bilateral agreements, enhancing trade and cooperation in other fields. This would help India with assured energy security because pipeline projects are risky so long as they pass through Pakistan.

References

1. Talmiz Ahmad. Implications for India's energy security. *In* Noronha, Ligia and Sudarshan, Anant, ed. India's energy security. London: Routledge, 2009. p. 64–86.

2. McKinsey 2005 In A historic beginning for Asian oil economy, (proceedings of the First Rounda Table), Ministry of Petroleum and Natural Gas, Government of India. pp. 83.

3. Persian Gulf Oil and Gas Export Fact Sheet. Energy Information Agency (EIA), Dept of Energy, Washington, DC.

4. ECSSR, 2007, Economic security issues and the role of the Gulf energy sector. In Gulf oil and gas–ensuring economic security. Abu Dhabi : The Emirates Centre for Strategic Studies and Research, p 11.

5. Ernest & Young, 2006. *In* New vistas for regional cooperation in Asian oil economy, (proceedings of the second round table), Ministry of Petroleum and Natural Gas, Government of India, pp 94.

6. EIA, 2007. Country analysis briefs : Caspian Sea. Energy Information Administration, US Department of Energy, Washington, DC.

7. Govt of India, 2001. Report of the group on India hydrocarbon vision – 2025. In Jasjit Singh (ed), Oil and gas in India's security. New Delhi : Knowledge World. Pp 131-230.

8. Integrated Energy Policy : Report of the Expert Committee. New Delhi : Planning Commission, 2006.

9. Talmiz Ahmad. Implications for India's energy security. In Noronha, Ligia and Sudarshan, Anant, ed. India's energy security. London :Routledge, 2009. p. 69–70

10. Ibid

11. Ibid

12. Dixit, J. N. 2004. Emerging international security environment :Indian perceptions with focus on South Asian and Central Asian predicaments. InSanthanam K and Dwivedi, R (eds), India and Central Asia–advancing the common interest. New Delhi: Anamaya Publishers, pp 19–20.

13. Varadarajan, S. 2006. Energy key in the new Asian architecture. The Hindu, New Delhi, January 25, 2006.

14. Roy, M S, 2006. The Shanghai cooperation organization: a critical evaluation. IDSA Strategic Comments. IDSA, July 4, 2006.

15. Aiyar, M S, 2005. Inaugural address at the 'Round Table of Asian Ministers on Regional Cooperation in the Oil Economy Stability, Security, Sustainability through Mutual Interdependence, January 5, 2005, New Delhi. In A historic beginning for Asian oil economy, Ministry of Petroleum and Natural Gas, Govt of India, pp. 10–11.

16. Ernst & Young. 2006. Presentation at the Ministerial Round Table on Cooperation between North and Central Asian Producers and Principal Asian Consumers regarding Stability, Security & Sustainability in Asian hydro carbon Economy, 25 Nov 2005.

17. APS 2006 'The Caspian Sea - The History & Legal background' APS review, 34th year, July 3-10, 2006.

Chapter –6

Gas without Borders : India's Gas Pipelines, Geopolitics and Pipeline Diplomacy

Introduction

In 2009 India was the fourth largest consumer of energy in the world. Its GDP in 2013 has fallen to 5.5 per cent per annum. And, its energy demand is expected to grow around 5 to 6 percent per annum. As a result of the available estimates, the consumption of energy is going to double in 12 to 13 years. As a result of these estimates India is currently the fourth largest energy consumer in the world. With its GDP projected to grow at eight percent per annum, energy demand is expected to rise to around five to six percent per annum, which in effect, means doubling of current consumption in about 12 to 13 years. While coal has been the major component of India's energy basket, gas which currently at around nine percent could well grow to about 15 to 20 percent, if India is able to meet the demand. Gas supply is currently around 100 MMSCMD which includes both domestic gas and liquefied natural gas (LNG) and once gas is freely available the demand for the fuel is likely to rise appreciably. Presently, the fertilizer and power sectors are the major consumers of gas at 29 percent and 40 percent respectively with the balance being consumed in industrial and domestic sectors. With large gas discoveries in the KG Basin off India's south eastern coast, the domestic gas position is likely to improve considerably but the need will continue.

In 2010 India was the world's fifth largest importer of oil importing more than 2.2 mbpd. India's crude oil imports bill for 2011–12 was $150 billion.

India has three LNG terminals on its west coast and is in the process of constructing a fourth one, which will be commissioned by end 2012. Three transitional pipeline proposals listed below, have been conceptualised from time to time but for various reasons have either stalled or are making very limited progress. These include the Iran–Pakistan–India gas pipeline, the Myanmar–India gas pipeline and Turkmenistan–Afghanistan–Pakistan–India gas pipeline. Furthermore, the Oman–India subsea gas pipeline an idea once considered dead has been resurrected. The following is the status of each pipeline project along with pending issues that need to be looked into.

The Iran–Pakistan–India Gas Pipeline

The idea of Iran–Pakistan–India gas pipeline was initiated by Dr R K Pachauri, Director General, TERI, and Dr A S Ardekani of Iran in 1989. Iran holds the second largest gas reserves in the world and it would be appropriate if the supply of gas to India was channelised through a pipeline. The main problem in executing this pipeline project was that the pipeline had to pass through Pakistan. As relations between India and Pakistan have not remained cordial, it is always felt that Pakistan could interfere and stop the flow of the gas to India at anytime. Although the Indus water treaty between the two countries had operated very smoothly, the reason for that mainly was that Pakistan was more interested in the treaty. In this case the risks

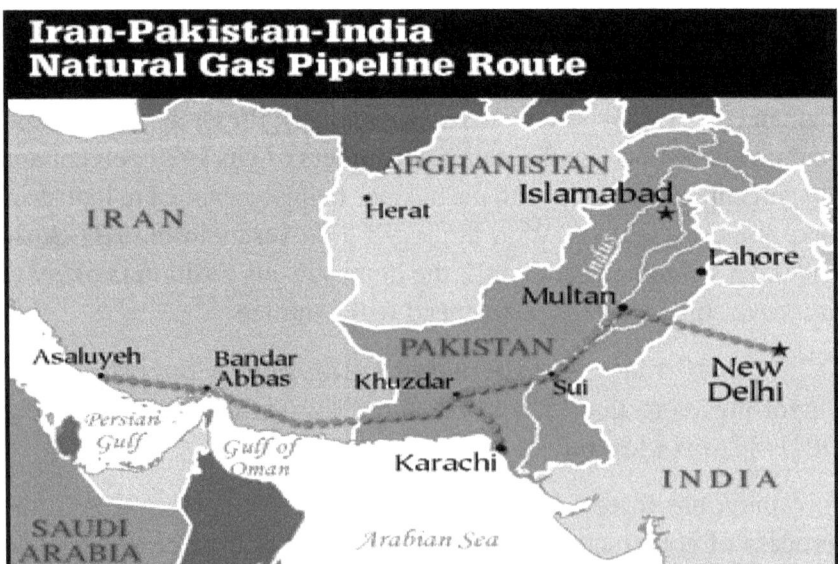

Iran-Pakistan-India Natural Gas Pipeline Route

are more as the relations between the two countries have remained strained because of Kashmir and related reasons.

Pakistan has begun to realize that it will soon be running short of gas, and may look into the project from the commercial and strategic points of view. The first detailed assessment of the project by Anglo–Australian company BHP Billiton was made in the year 2003. As conceived by BHP Billiton, a 44–inch pipeline was to be laid from Asalouyeh on the Iranian coast where gas from South Pars field would be pumped 1,115 kilometers across Iranian territory to the Pakistan border and a further 760 kilometers through Pakistan to the Indian border, At a distance 70 kilometers short of Indian borders the pipeline would link up with Pakistan's own gas network, the Sui Northern Gas Pipeline Ltd.as well as its southern counterparts before entering India. In India a further 600 kilometers pipeline could be laid to connect with the major west–north transmission line. It was anticipated that at its full capacity Pakistan would use about 60 MMSCMD and India 90 MMSCMD. The total cost of the project was estimated at $4 billion.

Since Pakistan could consider strategic and commercial interest in the project but its internal situation is volatile to the extent that any agreement with India will increase militancy in the country. In 2004 India's security concerns had abated as it was considered that Pakistan had a stake in the smooth operation of the pipeline. India's formal commitment to the project was made by Prime Minister, Dr Manmohan Singh, in September 2004. Despite the unrest in Baluchistan where Pakistan's own gas lines from the Sui Gas fields were regularly blown up by the insurgents, it was felt that the project could go forward, provided certain measures were taken to physically protect the pipeline and if breached to repair it quickly and at a short notice.

Since 2004, while discussions on bilateral or trilateral bases between the three countries made some progress, there have also been road blocks and changes in the base numbers and costs. First BHP Billiton revised the cost to $7 billion because of increase in steel price and increase in diameter of the pipeline. Then it was rumored that Pakistan is demanding a transit fee of as high as $700 million, though this was subsequently denied. Also the contracts to be concluded with

Iran especially a pipeline contract will need to be approved by the Supreme Economic Council. Iran would support the deal if India did not support the U.S. as the relations between Iran and the U.S. have been deteriorating.

Iran had proposed that each country should build its own section of pipeline; not a very satisfactory arrangement in terms of operation of the entire network, obtaining international finance and gaining the confidence of customers in terms of reliability of supply despite three years having passed, in a meeting in May 2008 India and Pakistan couldn't come to an agreement on transit and transportation fees. Meanwhile there has been a change on the Iranian side. It has laid a pipeline IGAT–7, for domestic use from Asalouyeh to the eastern town of Iranshahar, which will be extended 100 kilometers to the Pakistan border to meet Pakistan and India's requirements. The spare capacity of this pipeline is 60 MMSCMD and therefore the availability stands reduced to 30 MMSCMD for each country. In the case of India this is one–third of what was originally planned and considerably diminishes the importance of the pipeline, unless its capacity is augmented later to restore the supply to the original figure. Through all these developments, the cost of the pipeline continues to be touted at $7 billion despite its length in Iran having been reduced by about 1000 kilometres

In constructing the pipeline, Iran's contribution will be restricted to extending the IGAT–7 pipeline by just 100 kilometers. Pakistan will carry the biggest risk as the capacity of its section of pipeline will need to meet India's as well as its own requirement i.e 60 MMSCMD. In view of the developments discussed above, the Iran–Pakistan–India gas pipeline proposal is in the limbo.

Myanmar–India Gas Pipeline

The A1and A3 blocks in the Rankhine offshore area of Myanmar, near the port of Sittve have gas reserves between 160 to 280 BCM, as estimated by Gaffney Cline and Associates. India's share in these blocks is 30 percent, with a 20 percent participating interest held by ONGC Videsh Ltd. And 10 percent by Gas Authority of India. Kogas of Korea holds 10 percent while Daewoo of South Korea is the operator with 60 percent interest.

In February 2004, a letter of intent was issued to GAIL making it the preferential buyer of the gas from block A. In March 2006, a MoU was signed reinforcing that GAIL would be a preferential buyer of natural gas from Myanmar but at the same time a similar MoU was signed with China. Earlier in January 2005, India had signed a bilateral agreement with Myanmar to import gas through Bangladesh. However Bangladesh insisted that other bilateral issues be discussed with India, including trade imbalances and transit of electricity to which India did not agree. As a result Bangladesh did not allow the pipeline to be laid through its territory. India then examined the possibility of laying much longer line from Myanmar through India's north eastern states. GAIL separately also examined the possibility of compressing the gas (CNG) and moving it in ships to an Indian port. Around that time Myanmar also invited bids for export of gas inform of LNG but the proposal was not acted upon with any great seriousness as the gas reserves did not justify this option.

In January 2006 Myanmar advised India of China's intention to buy the gas and in February 2007 it was agreed that the entire production of 16 MMSCMD of gas from A1 and A3 fields will be sold to Petro China at a wellhead price of $4.279/MMBtu. China is to lay a 2,380 kilometer pipeline connecting the gas field to Kunming in China and beyond. China was also to pay $150 million annually for 30 years as a transit fee for the 990 kilometer through Myanmar.

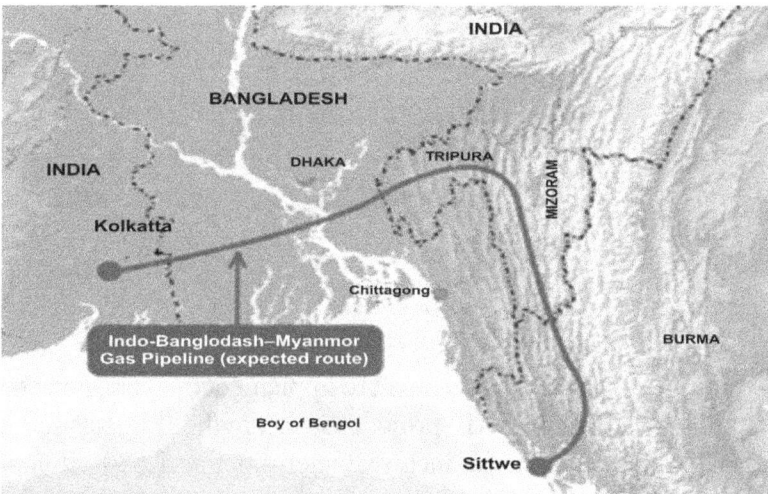

Indo-Banglodash–Myanmor Gas Pipeline (expected route)

The award of gas contract to china was attributed to China having vetoed a draft resolution tabled in UN Security Council to ease repression and release political prisoners in Myanmar. Though this may well be the case, there is no doubt that India lost considerable time looking at various options, carrying out feasibility reports etc. Equally, it is not difficult to see that this contract has strategic and security value for China as, apart from gas from Myanmar, the pipeline could, on some future date be used to ferry re gasified LNG terminal at Sittwe. It also opens up the possibility of laying a parallel oil pipeline to transship oil from the Middle East and avoid the long haul through the Straits of Malacca. It is not surprising that china pulled out all stops to secure this contract.

Turkmenistán–Afghanistan, Pakistan–India Gas Pipeline

The laying of the gas pipe line from southern Turkmenistan through Afghanistan to Pakistan was proposed by an Argentinian company, Bridas in 1992. Due to the US presence in the area, the project was re–allocated to an American company, Unocal which later pulled out of the project because of the very unstable conditions in Afghanistan.

The project was revived in the year 2002 when the heads of state of three countries signed an agreement to implement the Turkmenistan–Afghanistan–Pakistan (TAP) project. Gas from the Dauletabad field was to be fed through a 56–inch diameter pipeline,1,680 kilometer in length, and with the capacity of 90 MMSCMD to Pakistan via Herat and Kandahar in Afghanistan to join up with Pakistan's local gas network. The Asian Development Bank (ADB) was appointed the main development partner to facilitate the project, to serve as an honest broker. The cost of the project was estimated at $3. 3billion. A number of steering committee meetings were held under the aegis of ADB to discuss the project but the details of the project could not be finalized. It was felt hat for the project to be viable, it should be extended to India to link up with the transmission line feeding gas to northern India. Initially India agreed to be an observer and decided to become a member only in 2010, after which the project was re named as the Turkmenistan–Afghanistan–Pakistan–India (TAPI) pipeline project. As a result the cost has now got escalated to over $7 billion. India's stated reluctance has been that it was not sure that the gas reserves in Daultabad could service the requirements of all the three countries for next 30 years. It seems India is not satisfied with the unstable political and security situation in Afghanistan and related security fears. The reserves feeding the TAPI pipeline were originally estimated at 1.7TCM by a Russian Geologists. In an audit carried out by DeGolyer and MacNaughton along with Gaffney Kline in 2003, the estimated reserves were raised to 4.5 TCM more than sufficient to meet a demand of 90 MMSCMD over 30 years. Nonetheless in 2008 Gaffney Kline was asked to make an independent assessment of all of the country's gas reserves. Till 2013 there has not been any progress in the project.

Present Status

Indian cabinet on 18 May 2012 approved the model agreement for buying the Turkman gas that would be wheeled across Afghanistan and Pakistan through a $7.6 billion pipeline. The Turkman gas would cost $10–$12 per unit in India including transit fee and transportation charges. The transit fees has been fixed at 50 cents per unit and would be same for Afghanistan and Pakistan. Gas is scheduled to flow from 2016.

Originally Turkmenistan proposed to supply gas from its Dauletabad Field but now it will come from South Yolotan field. Global energy consultants Gaffney Kline has estimated the reserves at between 13 and 21 trillion cubic meters. The 1735 km pipeline would run from southeastern Turkmenistan into Afghanistan then parallel to highway from Herat to Kandhar and finally via Quetta and Multan in Pakistan to Fazilka in India.

Oman–India Sub–Sea Natural Gas Pipeline

In 1995, the Oman OIL Company headed by John Duess proposed laying a 1,100 kilometer subsea pipeline of 24–inch diameter that would link Oman Gas fields to a landfall point in the state of Gujarat in India. Advantages of this proposal included the short distance and the fact that no transit through a third country was involved. However the proposal could not be materialized as, first there were technology problems manufacturing a pipe thick enough to withstand the water pressure at depths of 3500 meters; second no submarine vessel has been developed to repair the pipeline at the depth if required; and third, the strong ocean currents in the sea bed could affect the stability of the pipeline. Finally India felt that reserves of gas in Oman would not be sufficient to sustain delivery over a period of 30 years.

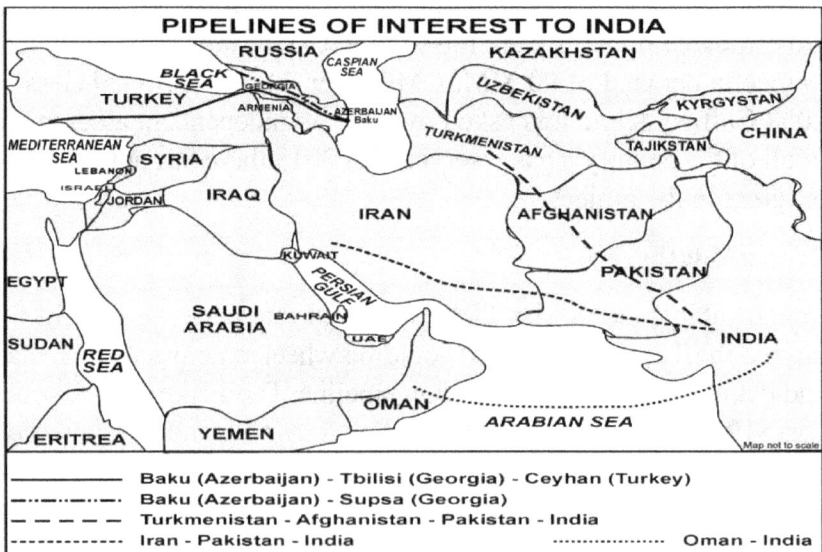

PIPELINES OF INTEREST TO INDIA

Baku (Azerbaijan) - Tbilisi (Georgia) - Ceyhan (Turkey)
Baku (Azerbaijan) - Supsa (Georgia)
Turkmenistan - Afghanistan - Pakistan - India
Iran - Pakistan - India   Oman - India

The South Asian Gas Enterprises (SAGE) whose key team members were associated with the original project has confirmed that the earlier technical difficulties have now been overcome. Corus, the UK Steel Company recently acquired by Tata Steel of India, now has the technology to manufacture the steel pipeline for the project. It has won a contract to supply a 312–kilometers length of pipeline of the required specification, to be laid on the seabed in Gulf of Mexico for the Per dido North Project at the depths of up to 3900 meters.

SAGE is planning to create an energy corridor, with several pipelines connecting energy producing countries like Iran, Turkmenistan, Qatar, and making the pipelines pass through the UAE and Oman, all the way to India, Lately in 2012 SAGE was negotiating gas supplies from Turkmenistan, Iran and Qatar.

Heerema, the Netherlands–based marine engineering contractor has developed a new barge that can lay pipelines at that depth. SAGE maintains that no deep water large diameter pipeline has ever required in–situ repairs, nonetheless remote operated repair system have been developed over the last five years, but will take time to carry out repairs. SAGE considers that by providing two lines, with a built in redundancy factor, the need for repairs will not arise. SAGE has therefore proposed to lay two 28 inch lines each of which would carry 31.5 MMSCMD gas to India the project cost is estimated at between $2.1 to 3.4 billion for the first line, SAGE has suggested that the gas sellers and buyers could be the owners of the pipeline and could set the tariff, which is expected not to exceed $1.30/MMBtu with the commissioning of the second line.

The developments suggest that the project could be feasible technically. Yet the technical feasibility of the proposal as well as the cost estimates will need to be addressed in detail. Presentations have been made to various ministries of government of India. Because of the earlier concern regarding Oman's gas reserves there is the need to develop the land based gas pipe linkages on the Arabian peninsula with other countries in order to augment the supply of gas to India through this route

Analysis and Conclusion

India is surrounded by countries that have abundant gas reserves, but because of security and political considerations India has not been able to finalise any overseas pipeline project so far. Infrequent meetings with the concerned countries with long gaps have confirmed that unless security and political issues are resolved there is less hope of finalizing an agreement. Iran–Pakistan–India gas pipeline project has suffered because of these reasons and the proposed transportation and transit fees proposed by Pakistan. While the nuclear deal with USA was being negotiated, India seemingly did not want to offend USA and therefore stalled discussions on the pipeline by highlighting but not moving forward on these two issues which in terms of total gas supply cost were relatively minor items. China's lately expressed willingness to come on board and become a partner in the proposal has been welcomed by Pakistan and Iran. While it is seen as an effort to get India to move faster in the matter, China factor needs to be taken more seriously. Considering the extent to which it is prepared to pipe gas over long distances as in the case of Turkmenistan and Myanmar. It is not inconceivable that a pipeline could be laid from Pakistan along the Karakoram highway and through the Karakoram pass into western China. China would be too pleased to get the access to the vast gas reserves of Iran.

In the case of Myanmar pipeline India lost various options and was perceived as a slow mover. Also it would appear that complacency set in with GAIL being initially nominated as the sole marker of the gas. China stepped in fast and for the reasons discussed earlier, was able to wrest the project away from India.

India has recently been discussing the Turkmenistan–Afghanistan– India pipeline project. Of the two pipeline proposals from Iran and Turkmenistan, the later has already fructified. Iran can easily supply the relatively small quantity of 60 MMSCMD to Pakistan and India ; second there is only one transit country for India as opposed to two for the Turkmenistan pipeline (the greater the number of transit countries the more complex the negotiations.); third, Pakistan has equal stake in the quantity of gas to be supplied by Iran; fourth, the democratic government in Pakistan is better placed than its predecessor to tackle and quell the unrest in Baluchistan province through which the pipeline will pass. Finally, once the pipeline becomes operational it should also be possible to increase its capacity. For this to happen India will need to move more decisively and quickly than it has in the past to sew up the deal, inspite of the US pressure.

The Oman–India pipeline proposal is a resurrection of an earlier one. As it is one of the world's deepest subsea proposals, India will need to be satisfied as to the proposed technology as well as competence of the South Asian Gas Enterprise and associated organizations. If these are clearly established the project has the best chance of being implemented as the economies look good no transit is involved and security risks are minimal.

The advantages of receiving gas from Iran, Turkmenistan and Oman is that it will result in a more balanced internal distribution of the gas in India than would otherwise be the case, leading to savings in transportation costs. Currently it is planned to move K G basin gas all the way to the north. Gas from Iran and Turkmenistan could feed the north, LNG terminals and Omani gas could feed the west and south with the KG basin gas feeding the west, south and east.

The unresolved issues of all the long pending pipeline proposals has been the diffidence of the government of India to negotiate upfront the well– head price of the gas, while spending an inordinate amount of time on gas reserves, pipeline alignments, transportation and transit fees, and security issues. With no commitment on prices, the supplying countries have enjoyed the benefit in the last few years of rising international gas prices. Also increases in steel prices have led to the doubling of cost of pipeline infrastructure. What has held India back is, first, the low price of domestic gas, which makes market based prices of gas look expensive, second inability of the power sector to raise electricity prices, instead being required to provide cheap power to the agricultural sector(thus resulting in high commercial losses); and the third, the higher subsidies that will be given to the fertilizer sector if gas prices are increased.

India's long term energy needs require that it accesses all energy forms from multiple sources and enhance its energy security. Success in importing gas by pipeline from neighboring countries will depend on how India uses its economic strategies that will attract Pakistan to support and secure the flow of oil and gas through its territory from

Iran and Central Asia. India should rise to blend well its foreign policies with its economic strategies especially in case of energy security issues.

References

1. Batra, Ravi Kumar. Natural gas pipelines : geopolitics, affordability, security dimensions. *In* In Noronha, Ligia and Sudarshan, Anant, ed. India's energy security. London : Routledge, 2009. p. 87–96.

2. Airy, A. 2005. Myanmar offers well–head gas at $2.52/MMBtu. *Financial Express.* August 18, 2005.

3. Airy, A, 2008. Pipe dream : India, Pak agree to disagree on transit, transport fees. *Financial Express.* May 7, 2008.

4. Analysis 'China and Turkmen energy'. *United Press International.* January 4, 2008.

5. Analysis 'UK firm to audit Turkmen gas'. *United Press International,* March 28, 2008.

6. Batra, R. 2007. Gas without borders. *Hardnews,* 4(7), pp 33–35.

7. Chatterji, S. 2008. Govt goes slow on IPI pipeline. *Business Standard.*

8. India join wins mega gas pipeline project. *The Economic Times.* April 25, 2008.

9. Mohan, N C. 2008. Turkmenistan deal revives Iran hopes. *Hindustan Times,* April 26, 2008.

10. Myanmar ditches India for China in gas deal. *Times of India,* April 9, 2007.

11. Myanmar gas blocks award to China, a setback for India. *Economic Times,* May 1, 2007.

12. Myanmar gas for China : PMO wants petroleum ministry to try again. www. indianpetro.com

13. Ranjan, A. 2007. Myanmar gas bid lost, MEA and petroleum in war of words. *The Indian Express,* July 30, 2007.

14. Siddiqui, H. 2005. Turkmenistan gas reserves inadequate. *The Financial Express,* February 18, 2005.

15. Subramanian, N. 2008. Accord on TAPI gas pipeline project. *The Hindu,* April 25, 2008.

Chapter –7

International Choke Points, Secure Routes and Supply of Energy to India

Introduction

India's energy security is vulnerable in the given circumstances. India needs to have multiple and diverse energy partners and also should have secure and reliable routes for the supply of its energy import. As India depends on the import of energy it is prone to disruptions. The securing of shipping routes (for oil, coal and LNG) or pipelines for oil and natural gas is as important as the security of equity investments and trade with energy–rich countries. In case of bilateral energy trade and equity investments, the stability of the source countries is also of utmost importance. Further, the security of oil installations and key transportation routes and pipelines is equally important. It is for this reason that the security of transportation routes is being discussed in this chapter. Transportation routes are open to risks and threats from more than one country, given the transitional nature of shipping lanes and pipelines, as well as the physical disruption caused by natural disasters, accidents and traffic constrictions at maritime chokepoints. [1]

This chapter highlights some of the risks and vulnerabilities that India faces vis–a vis the physical supply of energy from its key energy partners. Although the transportation infrastructure and vulnerabilities within India's borders is an equally important aspect of ensuring India's energy security, this chapter will focus on the external transportation routes. To this end, the chapter identifies the threats that make India's routes insecure and the response mechanism India has already put in place to deal with some of these risks. It also highlights possible mechanism that India should push for in order to circumvent some of the vulnerabilities that its energy routes face.

Types of Risks to Energy Supply Routes

Given that India has to meet a growing proportion of its demand for energy in the coming years through imports, the security of supply routes is an integral aspect of country's energy security strategy. India's commercial energy basket is dominated by coal (53%); oil (31%); and gas (8%). Given the limited domestic availability of coal, oil, and gas, energy import dependency for India in the future is projected to rise to 70%, 94% and 24% in 2031, up from 14%, 74% and 21% for coal, oil and gas respectively in 2001. [2] India has limited domestic reserves of uranium as well. According to the IEP (Integrated Energy Policy), India's reserves of uranium can only power about 10000 MW of expansion PHWR (pressurized heavy water reactors). Furthermore, given the low quality of uranium ore available in India, supplying nuclear energy from domestic resources is up to 2 to 3 times costlier than if it were sourced by international supplies (Planning Commission) India will therefore be dependent on uranium imports in the short to medium term. [3]

Securing routes for imported energy for India, based on its projected need for imported energy, pertain mainly to maritime sea lanes or what are referred to as Sea Lanes of Communications (SLOC). Transportation routes are vulnerable to several types of threats. These threats can be broadly grouped into three categories–

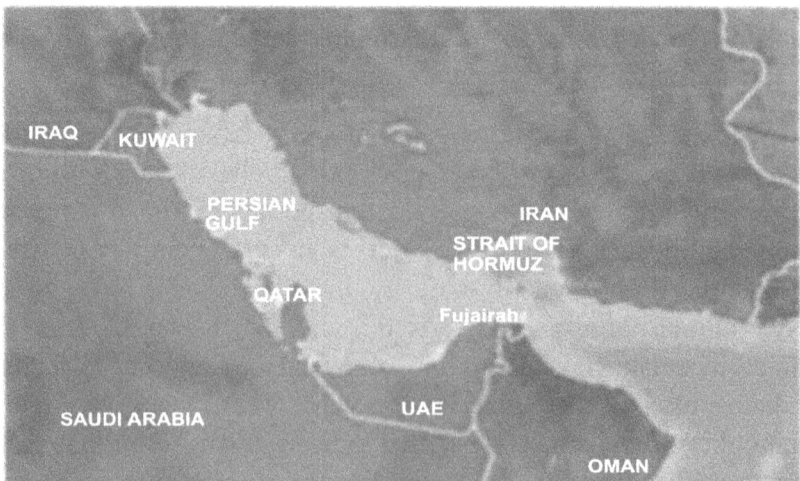

Source : EIA

(i) international disputes (ii) intra–state conflicts and piracy, and (iii) natural disasters and natural chokepoints.

International Disputes

Conflict between the countries can be a source of instability for sea lanes that need to pass through regions which would fall within the ambit of that conflict for India. The route that is most vulnerable to being blocked due to deteriorating relations between countries at the international level is the route that passes through the Strait of Hormuz. The Strait is about 21 miles wide at its narrowest point and the daily flow of oil through it is about 7–17 million barrels which is roughly 40% of all the seaborne traded oil (or 20% of oil traded worldwide)

Any blockage or threat to the security of the Strait of Hormuz is capable of blocking anywhere from 30% to 65% of India's oil imports from Iraq, Kuwait, Qatar, the UAE, Iran and Saudi Arabia, depending on whether the load ports are located on the Persian Gulf and have to pass the Strait of Hormuz or not.

To be sure a blockade or a blockage at the Strait of Hormuz is not only a challenge for India but also for the rest of the oil importing world. Also, given that oil importing countries need markets, a blockade would also affect oil exporting countries of West Asia. In this scenario therefore, how real is the threat of blockade at Strait of Hormuz?

The possibility of an actual blockade is indeed slim, but the vulnerability of the strait to a conflict between Iran and the west (particularly the US) is very real as was evident in the recent past. Iran's continued noncompliance with UN Security Council resolutions, to stop enriching the uranium had led to heightened tensions in the region. While Iran threatened to respond to any military attack by either striking Israel or 'burning down 'America's vital interests around the globe if the US or Israel launched a military strike on Iran's nuclear facilities. American, British and Bahraini ships were involved in joint exercises – "Stake Net" to protect their oil and gas installations in the region. However under President Obama's new policy to engage Iran and a deal brokered by IAEA to persuade

Iran to ship Iran's low–enriched uranium (LEU) for conversion 20% enriched uranium to fuel a medical research reactor in Tehran have helped lessen the tension. Nonetheless, relations between the two remain difficult. Depending on deteriorating relations between the two, strategists warn that Iran could lay mines or increase its submarine activity–activate all that are well within Iran's growing littoral warfare capabilities. [5] As the India–US strategic partnership becomes stronger, a possible eruption of hostilities between the US and Iran might impede discussions on Iran–Pakistan–India pipeline.

Intra– State Conflict, Terrorism and Piracy

Shipping routes as well as pipelines are also vulnerable to attack from international conflicts, that is, discord between governments and secessionists groups as well as non–state actors such as terrorists groups and pirates. The pirates and extremist groups pose a very real threat to supply routes that need to traverse regions marked by intra–state conflict. The inter–linkages between crime, piracy and intra–state conflict make it difficult for states to individually deal with threats to SLOC's merely through reactive military means that do not address the root cause of the conflict.

India's energy imports that pass through the Malacca Straits and the Bab–al–Man dab or round the Gulf of Aden are most vulnerable to pirate attacks. In 2007 there were a reported 263 pirate attacks, particularly in unpatrolled waterways through which 90% of the global trade flows. Piracy attacks hit a high in 2009–The International

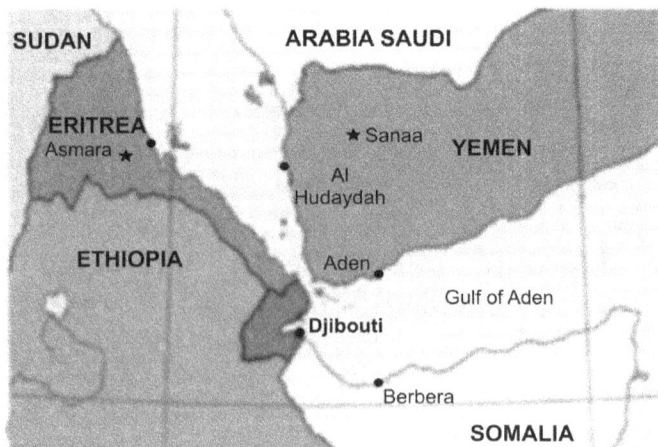

Maritime Bureau's Piracy Reporting Centre in Malaysia reported that pirates attacked 42 oil–laden tankers around the world alone. A 40% rise from 2008. In 2010 itself there were three successful piracy attacks–Two around the Gulf of Aden and one in Malacca Strait. [6]

Over 200 ships and half of the world's oil and two thirds of the world's LNG pass through the Malacca Straits. Not only piracy, but terrorist outfits and dissatisfied insurgent groups operating in the region make the straits a particularly insecure and risky SLOC for energy imports. For India disruptions due to pirate attacks in Malacca Straits would affect India's current imports of coal from Indonesia (non–coking coal from Kalimantan) and natural gas imports from Malaysia. As India seeks to diversify its energy imports, disruptions caused by pirate attacks in the Malacca Straits could impact the country's

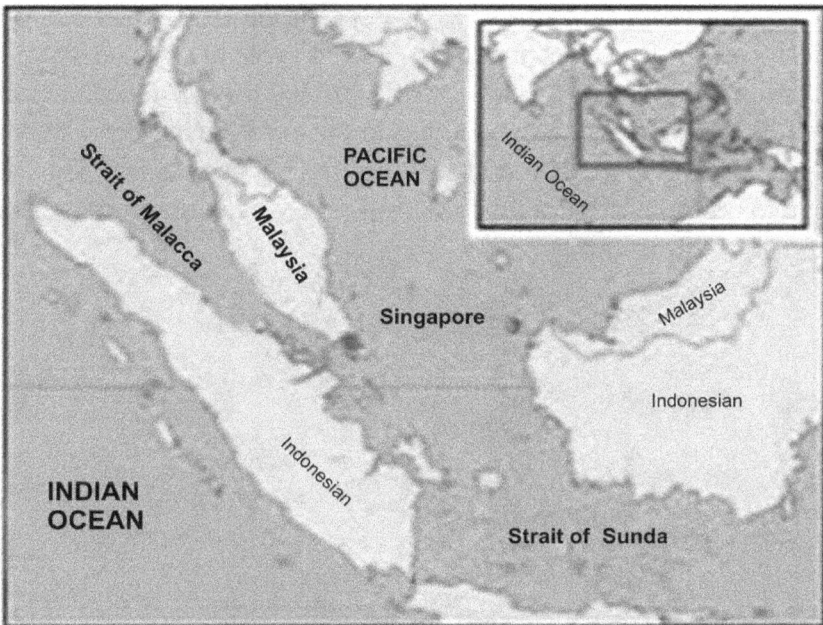

energy imports from the countries such as Vietnam (for coal), and Indonesia for natural gas as well as coal. At its narrowest, the strait is merely 1.7 miles–making passing tankers a ready target for thefts and hijacking, particularly because these tankers are slow–moving and difficult to manoeuvre. Given the inflammable nature of LNG, vessels carrying LNG are considered to be even more vulnerable to the terrorist hijackings. The Bab–Al Man dab poses another serious threat to energy imports, not only for India, but the world at large. Situated between Yemen, Djibouti and Eritrea, the strait of Bab–Al Man dab provides a strategic link between the Mediterranean Sea and Indian Ocean and connects the Red Sea and the Gulf of Aden and the Arabian Sea. Bab–Al Man dab is only 18n miles wide and tanker traffic is limited to a two mile wide channel. The chokepoint at Bab–al Man dab has the potential of constricting / hampering India's energy imports from North Africa, although that is minimal as compared to India's imports from the West Asia. However as India casts it's net wider in search of newer energy partners, particularly in Africa, the Bab–Al Man dab may well pose a challenge to India's oil imports from Sudan, Algeria, Libya and Egypt and LNG imports from Europe. (Belgium and Norway). [7]

Piracy in Gulf of Aden has been persistent threat over the last decade or so. However, the threat has only recently gained serious attention, particularly energy security in 2008 for instance, a total of 135 attacks took place resulting in 44 ships having been seized by pirates and more than 600 seafarers having been kidnapped and held for ransom. [8] Pirates functioning from the failed state of Somalia

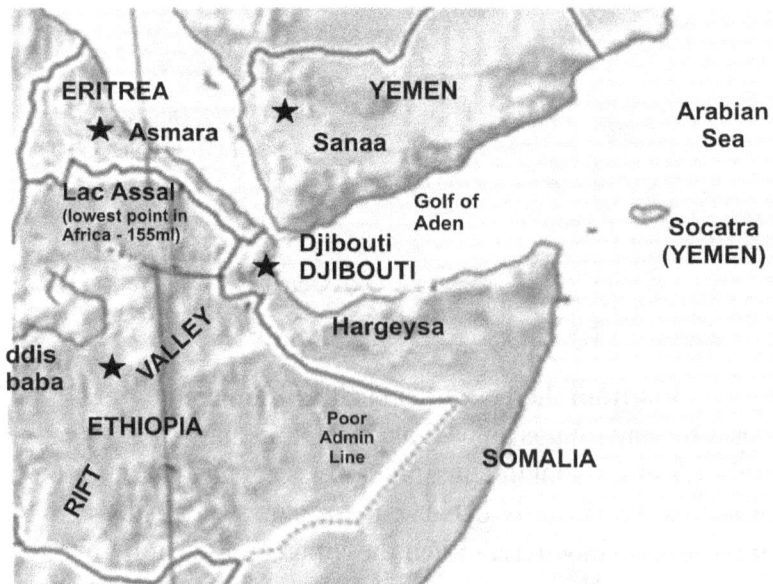

were behind the hijacking of supertanker MV Sirius Star about 450 nautical miles off the coast of Kenya in November. The Saudi owned ship, Sirius Star was loaded with 2 billion barrels of crude oil, worth about US$110 million. The high jacking of the Sirius Star was the first most direct instance of the impact of piracy on the security of energy supplies in the world.

Natural Disasters and Choke points

The supply of oil coal and natural gas can also be disrupted by the concurrence of natural disasters, like hurricanes and tsunamis. The sudden nature of such transitional disasters makes all countries vulnerable to supply disruptions and sudden oil spikes due to disruptions, the 2005 Hurricane Katrina that struck the Gulf of Mexico, for instance dealt a heavy blow to a major part of the America's energy Infrastructure; and as a consequence caused a surge in energy crises.

In the Indian Ocean too, there has been concern for studying the possible impact of natural disasters such as typhoons, cyclones and tsunamis on the energy security of the littoral countries. The Tsunami of 2004 caught all Asian countries unprepared. However, in its wake it raised the need for emergency preparedness and early warning systems. Since 2004 therefore, countries of the region have been working towards putting in place institutions that would make Information sharing and coordination between the Indian Ocean countries transparent and seamless.

Way Forward–Possible Response Options

India's unique geo–strategic location at the head of the Indian Ocean with an extensive EEZ (Exclusive Economic Zone) poses challenges as well as opportunities for the country. The asymmetric maritime challenges and threats facing India have already resulted in significant bilateral maritime relations between India and several Southeast Asian countries as well as extra regional powers (US, Russia, Israel).

Joint Patrolling

The Indian Navy has collaborated with other countries in what is called a "sea lane sanitizing role." Countries such as Indonesia,

Singapore and Malaysia have looked to India as a 'reliable and non–controversial ally' in keeping SLOCs and chokepoints, such as Malacca Straits, clear of piracy and its linkages with terrorism. India already has a series of joint patrolling exercises with Indonesia' in a part of 200 nautical miles–long energy feeder path'[9]

A regional approach to securing SLOCs is however, crucial. There is a need to pool resources, assets, efforts and intelligence in order to tackle threats to maritime security such as the identification of suspicious vessels on high seas. [10] There are several regional multilateral foras in Asia that seek to address issues related to maritime security, for example the EAS (East Asia Summit), ARF (ASEAN Regional Forum), IONS (Indian Ocean Naval Symposium), the CSCAP (Council for Security Cooperation in the Asia Pacific) and ReCAPP (Regional Cooperation Agreement on Combating Piracy and Armed Robbery against ships in Asia). [11] The Indian Navy also holds an annual diplomatic initiative called Milan that is a comprehensive Track 1 exercise for greater coordination on issues of ocean governance, sea piracy, terrorism and disorder at sea. [12]

Patrolling is relevant not only on sea based routes, but also for land based pipelines. The security of transitional pipelines can be ensured, among other things, through patrolling of the entire length of the pipeline. This can ensure that pipelines are not attacked by secessionists groups/terrorists working in that area.[13]

Disaster Management

The Tsunami in 2004 brought to the fore the possibility of natural disasters disrupting the energy supplies in the region. Along with joint patrolling, countries are increasingly making disaster management and mitigation a crucial part of their maritime security, not least for securing their energy supplies. Early warning systems and easy flow of information can go a long way in alleviating the impact of natural disasters on energy supplies in the region

Alternative Routes

One way of circumventing threats to the existing transport routes is by identifying and pushing for alternative routes and mechanism that would allow India to Import its energy from routes that are relatively safer. Several of these alternative routes and mechanisms have already been discussed, but not become realities due to geopolitical reasons or due to the costs attached, for example the IPI and TAPI some of the other alternative routes are discussed below

Trans–Gulf Strategic Pipeline

To circumvent Strait of Hormuz, six possible alternative routes for a Trans–Gulf pipeline have been identified, which could bring oil from as far north as Iraq, passing through Kuwait, Saudi Arabia and United Arab Emirates (UAE) to the Omani capital Muscat on the Arabian Sea. Other possible routes could see the pipeline terminating in Yemen or Fujairah. One such route is the Dolphin project, which is a gas pipeline from Qatar to Fujairah. Another proposed pipeline would carry oil from the UAE's Habshan oil field, across the mountain range to the Emirate of Fujairah, located outside the Gulf of Oman. The most recent pipeline that is being discussed is under sea SAGE gas pipeline. The gas pipeline will stretch for 2000 km from Oman to India's western coast.

Another pipeline that has been suggested to give access to India to Central Asia oil via Israel is proposed by Turkey. The pipeline would circumvent the Suez Canal and make it possible to get oil from Central Asia to Cayhen in Turkey through pipelines, across the Mediterranean by tanker to Israel's port of Ashkelon and then onto India by pipeline or tankers.

Swap Arrangements

Apart from alternative routes, other mechanisms to ensure security of energy supplies and to circumvent difficult shipping or pipeline routes are swap arrangements. Swap arrangements allow countries to leverage their comparative advantages–that is proximity to an energy supplying country vis–à–vis overseas equity investments of another country. Recently India discussed the possibility of swap arrangements with Japan. As per this proposal, Japan could import gas from Sakhalin where India has equity stakes while India could gain access to Japan's gas supplies from West Asia. This arrangement would not only reduce transportation costs for both countries substantially, but would also help both Japan and India circumvent the Strait of Malacca. However this arrangement has not materialized, primarily due to Japan's reservations regarding the reliability of supplies from Russia. [14]

Treaties and Agreements

Another mechanism to ensure reliability of energy supplies is by putting in place bilateral and multilateral agreements. The ECT (Energy Charter Treaty) is a good example of ensuring the supplies of energy by providing a set of binding rules that 'protect long term energy investments, particularly those on transport infrastructure. These in turn provide security for long term supply agreements and protect the interests of energy producing , transit and consuming states alike '(ECT2008) India is considering joining up, at least as observers, this would make sense for India particularly considering the fact that important countries of West and Central Asia are also observers of ECT.

Conclusion

Secure routes for sustained and dependable energy supplies are an important constituent of the energy securing strategies of countries. The above mentioned strategies would have to be seen in conjunction with other efforts that are purely of domestic nature, such as building port and shipping infrastructures as well as building a strategic petroleum reserves.

Countries cannot secure routes on their own, unless the distance between them is short and they are contiguous. Otherwise, for considering shipping routes for oil, coal or LNG or pipelines for oil and PNG (Piped Natural Gas), there needs to be cooperation between countries to ensure routes are not attacked by pirates and terrorists, state and non–state actors, or impacted by environmental disasters and accidents.

References

1.   Sharma, Devika. Secure routes and the supply of energy to India. *Energy Security Insights.* Vol 4(4), October–December 2009, pp 21–26.

2. Building an energy secure future for India in consultation with stakeholders. New Delhi : TERI, 2010..

3. Planning Commission. 2006. Integrated Energy Policy.

4. EIA. 2008a. Strait of Hormuz.

5. Altman A. 2008. A brief history of pirates. Time, July 31, 2008

6. Talmadge C. 2008. Closing time, assessing the Iranian threat to the Strait of Hormuz. *International Security*, Vol 33(1) p. pp 82–117.

7. EIA. 2008.Bab el–Mandab.

8. International Maritime Organization. 2008. Piracy in waters off the coast of Somalia.

9. Dikshit, S. 2004. Malacca Straits security : role seen for Indian Navy. *The Hindu,* September 8, 2004. *y*

10. Khurana, G S. 2004. Maritime security in the Indian Ocean : convergence plus cooperation equals resonance. *Strategic Analysis*. Vol 28(3), July–September 2004, pp 411–426.

11. Sakhuja V. 2009. Combating terrorism in Asian waters. *Terrorism Monitor,* Vol 7(35), November 19, 2009.

12. Prabhakar W and Lawrence S. 2007. India's perspectives of Maritime Security. Paper presented at the 9th Asian Security Conference on Security Dynamics in Southeast Asia : Emerging Threats and Responses, February 9–10, 2007.

13. Batra, R K. 2008. Natural gas imports by pipeline : going nowhere. Hardnews. May 15, 2008.

14. Sibal K. 2007. No discussion on more nuclear reactors during Putin visit : Indian envoy.

Chapter –8

Maritime Dimension of India's Energy Security

India's Energy Demand Profile

The growing demand for natural gas and petroleum in India is because of various reasons including the dimensions of development. India's current commercial energy consumption is a mere 25% of the world average. About 73% of India's industrial energy needs are currently met by coal which are being replaced by natural gas and petroleum products. As the country's manufacturing sector develops further, the requirements of power generation will increase and lead to an increase in the demand for natural gas. [1]

The other reason for the increase in the demand for oil resources is due to the increase in the demand of public and freight transportation (sea, air and land). A number of private vehicles on Indian roads are getting added every day. Because of several such reasons, India's crude oil consumption during the last decade has grown by over 6% annually, which is twice the world average growth. [2] While its annual oil demand was 40 million tons a decade ago, it is now 135 million tons and is expected to increase to 370 million tons in next two decades. However the domestic production of crude oil has been stagnant and the current oil import dependence of 70 percent is likely to increase to 90% by 2030. [3] Growing dependency on external sources energy resources by India makes India's economy quite shaky.

Insular India

India's crude oil imports are all brought in by sea and in future supplies of natural gas may also be transported as Liquefied Natural Gas by sea. The options for overland natural gas pipeline are grim as such proposals have either been found unfeasible (technically or economically), or have faced political or security–based obstacles.

In terms of overland communications, India is bolted up within the subcontinent, which incidentally also bears its name. This has led to 97 percent of India's trade (by volume) being by sea, which is comparable to that of an island state. The barriers are posed by two important factors–first is natural topography (the highlands stretching across India's northern frontiers.) and second is political discord with Pakistan and Bangladesh. Russia and Central Asian republics (CAR) have emerged as the new petro states with ample natural gas reserves. However owing to the aforesaid barriers, their reserves are inaccessible to India despite their geographical proximity. It remains to be seen whether any one of the proposed gas pipelines will ever reach India but even if they materialize in the long term, most natural gas imports would still continue to arrive by sea.

In the case of domestic oil and natural gas, two third of domestic production is presently sourced from offshore locations in India's maritime zones, When the United Nations Convention on laws of sea, 1982 (UNCLOS–3) came into force in in November 1994, it provided regime of an Exclusive Economic Zone (EEZ) for all coastal states, extending to a distance of 200 nautical miles (nm) from the coast. Given the depletion of natural resources on land, this was a boon for all these states, and India was no exception. In fact considering its 7,500 kilometer long coast line, which is fifteenth longest in the world. India was given sovereign rights over an extensive maritime zone of 2.2 million sq km, which is nearly two thirds of its total land area. India's widespread island chains also contributed substantially to this large EEZ. The maritime zone around the Andaman and Nicobar Islands, for example makes up to 30 percent of India's total EEZ. Besides other resources, the seas under India's jurisdiction have provided some much needed oil and natural gas resources to India with a promise for more. [4]

Expanding Stakes

The offshore locations in India's EEZ account for two thirds of India's domestic production of oil and gas. They include Bombay High off western coast and various river basins off the eastern coast, such as the Krishna, Godavari, Cauvery and Mahanadi basins. Although the domestic production is small it is expected to rise if energy finds are located in Indian waters. However, the hydrocarbon potential of these offshore areas, which are mostly in the Bay of Bengal, is high considering the encouraging response of oil and gas companies so far. These offshore areas and extraction platforms are important from India's strategic and economic points of view. They are widely dispersed over 40,000 sq km of maritime area. At present the extracted oil and natural gas resources are mainly transported to refineries and consumers via submarine pipelines, since the distance involved is short and that the tankers are primarily used for coastal movement of refined products. We find that submarine pipelines are inherently secure in comparison to tankers, yet India may rely more on tankers in the future. The offshore areas of Andaman and Nicobar islands are said to possess the largest reserves of coal bed methane (CBM).[5] The ONGC has also identified prospective areas in the offshore Andaman and Laccadive ridge in the Arabian Sea containing natural gas hydrates. We thus see that offshore resources and products are likely to be transported to the mainland over significantly large transit distances, thereby necessitating the use of tankers/ shipping(since laying submarine may not be cost effective)

In case of India's imports of fossil fuel resources, more than 60% of crude oil is presently coming from West Asian (Middle East) region. While Saudi Arabia is India's largest supplier, the rest of the oil comes from other countries like Iran, Kuwait, Oman and the UAE. Some African states have also become India's major crude oil suppliers. Nigeria is currently India's second largest source of crude oil. A long term contract for LNG presently exists only with Qatar, but similar agreements need to be finalized soon with other countries like Algeria. India has also been resorting to spot buys of LNG, such as from Algeria and Egypt.

The import of oil from Africa was considered by India mainly not to depend heavily on West Asia. It had also been making efforts towards source diversification to the East. Indian oil and gas companies hold 45% stake in Vietnam's gas fields a majority (55 percent) stake in Australia and 20% stake in Myanmar's gas fields (all offshore). In case Myanmar's–India gas proposal seems unfeasible, India could resort to the gas being transported as LNG. A long term contract is being negotiated by India to import LNG from Malaysia.

In Russian Far East, OVL acquired a 20% stake in Exxon–Mobile–operated Sakhalin–I oil project. Plans are also afoot for OVL to export its share of natural gas from Sakhalin–I as LNG. ONGC and GAIL have jointly taken up 49% stake in Venezuelan oil fields. Crude oil supplies have since started arriving in India.

Coal will continue to constitute a major proportion of India's energy mix for many years India ranks third largest coal producer in the world only after China and USA. The shortfall between demand and domestic production is expected to be 105 million tons by 2012.

India's strategic interests over the past few decade have significantly expanded overseas, westwards and eastwards in terms of India's overall trade interactions with the world. This is true for its energy security as well. While geographical proximity to West Asia is an advantage due to the lower costs for oil and gas transportation, yet India is at a significant geo–strategic disadvantage when it comes to diversifying energy sources, since it is straddled between maritime choke points–the straits of Hormuz/Bab al Mandeb passage to the west; and the Southeast Asian straits to the east. In any case, West Asia will continue to be India's principle energy source.

It is important to note that most of the countries from which India's energy resources are sourced or where India has acquired energy stakes are plagued by geopolitical and social instabilities. In most cases this has a maritime security dimension since oil and gas fields are sited offshore. However, inherent political and financial risks in opting for these overseas investments were inescapable, India has been building close political ties with these resource rich countries since energy concerns have become an important element of foreign policy, but they may not suffice as insurance for its energy security.

Maritime Insecurities

Non State Threats

As India is predominantly dependent upon sea routes for its import of oil and gas, these sea routes are also predominantly getting insecure as a result of threats by non–state actors. Piracy and armed robbery of ships, in the Southeast Asian straits, and in East Africa, particularly off the coast of Somalia and the Gulf of Aden need greater attention and international cooperation in patrolling of the affected areas. It seems there has been improvement in the security of these areas but the risks are equally growing. As the examination of India's energy stakes indicates, much of Indian shipping that is carrying energy resources has to pass through these areas. The other areas, where piracy has spilled over from Southeast Asian waters westwards into Bay of Bengal or further east into South China Sea could also become a serious issue if not checked oat this stage.

The recent phenomenon of widespread terrorist attacks on ships by Islamic radicals have also increased substantially. Al Qeada is firmly entrenched in West Asia. Its rudimentary nautical expertise targeting stationary ships are using fast boats packed with explosives with USS Cole attack in October 2000. USS Cole bombing on October 12,2000 is an example. Using the same modus operandi the slow moving French tanker Limburg was attacked off Aden in October 2002. Soon thereafter, energy Infrastructure became the key targets of global terrorism as indicated by the events in Persian Gulf including the April 2004 Al Qaeda suicide attacks on Iraqi Al Basra and Khor–al–Amaya offshore oil terminals. Notwithstanding the presence of multinational naval forces, the Persian Gulf region continues to remain unstable. With 90% of oil exports from Persian Gulf being carried by sea the threat to the Gulf offshore platforms loading berths and oil /LNG tankers remains imminent.

Jammah Islamiyah, an offshoot of Al Qaeda is active in Southeast Asia and has been initiating separatist movements in various states like Indonesia, Philippines, and southern Thailand. Jammah Islamiyah aims to establish a pan–Islamic state in Southeast Asia. Separatist movements and Islamic fundamentalism creates clear regarding the shipping transport of energy supplies through the regional straits, In particular the Malacca strait. Malacca strait is the busiest of all, through which a quarter of the global trade passes aboard more than 62000 vessels every year, including half the world's oil and two thirds of its LNG. The terrorists are likely to use the nautical skill of the pirates to carry out attacks on shipping in the straits. It may not be practically possible for terrorists to capsize a large vessel at the most critical spot to block the Malacca strait but a major attack on hub–port ,a cruise liner or use of radiological weapons in the area would create sufficient impact on oil ship movements and severely disrupt global energy supplies.

If the global energy supplies get disrupted, there would be a direct impact on India's energy security. Hence the possibility of terrorists targeting India's energy lifelines cannot be discounted .Slow moving India–bound tankers could be the target for their bomb laden boats. Further, as April 2004 attacks by Al Qaeda on Iraqi oil terminals indicated, it would be even easier for the terrorists to attack fixed offshore installations in the EEZ such as oil extraction platforms using fast boats laden with explosives. The offshore rigs could be attacked by scuba divers and can use underwater scooter and limpet mines to destroy fixed installations.

Any maritime crimes in Indian waters contribute to the disorder at the sea and thereby increase the risk factor for India's offshore rigs and vessels that support the fuel extraction operations. Besides other crimes like drug trafficking, gun running and human smuggling persists. These drive internal instabilities and terrorism in Southeast Asian states and thus indirectly impinge upon the security of sea lines being used to transport energy resources.

The Vulnerabilities

India produced 880 thousand barrels per day in 2009–10 however it consumed 3 million bbl/d making it the fourth largest consumer of oil in the world. India needs a typical Very Large Crude Carrier (VLCC) of three lakh tons dead weight tonnage to carry about two million tons of oil. On an average about 40 shipments (including those carrying petroleum products) arrive in India every month. Considering the growth rate of six percent, the daily demand would nearly double to five million barrels by 2020, and considering a stagnant domestic productions which means a daily requirement of two VLCC equivalent loads of crude oil in 15 years. Added to these shipments are increasing shipments of LNG.

This situation exposes a number of vulnerabilities of India in the energy sector. First most of the vessels bring resources from West Asian and African states, where energy infrastructure (for both production and distribution) and transportation are at high risk due to prevailing Islamic fundamentalism, geopolitical instability or ethnic tensions.

Second the possibility of pirate attacks or any other mishap occurring on a vessel carrying Indian energy supplies has increased in direct proportion to the growing number of India bound vessels. These vessels also have to traverse pirate–infested areas, reaching India either through Gulf of Aden/ Somali waters (from the West), or through the Straits of Southeast Asia (from the East). With the increasing size of tankers driven by motives of economic profitability, the vulnerability of these vessels has increased significantly over the years. Terror strikes and boarding by the pirates have become relatively easy since the large tankers are now more cumbersome to maneuver and need to reduce speed while transiting restricted waters. Also these tankers cannot employ some of the latest technological advancement such as the secure ship (a 9000 volt electric fence installed around the ship to deter boarding by miscreants), due to nature of their inflammable cargos. It is therefore not surprising that the 4000–odd tankers plying the world's Oceans are victims in a quarter of pirate attacks, even though tankers constitute a mere 10%of the world shipping fleet.

The sea line extending from Arabian Peninsula to India also passes close to the coast of Pakistan, which makes vessels carrying India's strategic cargo extremely vulnerable to interdiction by Pakistani naval units during war time. China has provided technical and financial assistance to Pakistan to develop its Gwadar Port in Baluchistan Province sited very close to Strait of Hormuz. The facilities of this port are likely to be used by Chinese naval units.

India's domestic energy infrastructure in its maritime zones is also at risk since the offshore platforms/rigs and their supporting vessels and infrastructure are vulnerable to collisions and sabotage by terrorists and other elements that would like to hurt India's vital interests.

As per international law (UNCLOS–3), a state can establish a security and safety zone up to a maximum of 500 meters all around offshore installations and artificial islands in its EEZ. Within this zone, entry may be denied to all except authorized vehicles. However

UNCLOS–3 was signed in 1982 after three decades of negotiations and some of its provisions may not address the requirements of the current time. Five hundred meters of cushion is definitely inadequate to ensure security of offshore platforms today, considering that readily available modern commercial off–the–shelf technology has significantly enhanced the attacking capabilities of non–state actors including their use of high speeds of attack boats, effective communications for better coordination, the increasing lethality of weapons and explosives and even the easy availability of scuba gear and underwater scooters to carry out subsurface attacks.

The Way Ahead

Explore swapping options

India will be importing energy resources from the countries in South Eastern Asia. Passing of tankers through the insecure straits of South East Asia seems to be unavoidable. Some ways could be used to circumvent part of the unsafe routes unimpeded passage for ships that are transporting fossil fuel resources to India. One good way for India is to swap its energy imports that are sourced from West Asia and Africa, with those of the states in Eastern Asia which are sourced from within the region, particularly Indonesia, Malaysia and Australia. It may thus be worthwhile to explore the options and feasibility for entering into arrangements to exchange Indian oil Imports with those bound for China, Japan, South Korea or Taiwan. This would not only obviate the necessity for tankers to transit insecure stretches of sea lines but would also reduce transportation costs significantly. Off course this would be a part solution and not a comprehensive one.

Military Options

It may not be ideal for India to use its military forces to conduct expeditionary operations against a state to secure its energy assets and stake overseas there. However Indian forces may need to be prepared to provide security assistance to the countries that may request India's involvement. In case of an eventuality that might impinge on India's energy security, the role of Indian maritime forces would be crucial not only to transport men and material overseas to stabilize the situation overseas, but also to provide security to the offshore energy infrastructure and transportation.

Showcasing the military capabilities of Indian forces in a benign manner and providing security reassurance to the governments in these countries thus becomes an important aim of the periodical presence of Indian warships in foreign ports on goodwill missions and the naval power discharges its role as an instrument of foreign policy. Their mere presence close to foreign shores leads to the spread of nation's influence and political will to secure its vital interests and this in itself provides a measure of security. Hoever, another option for India would be develop strong bilateral relations with the oil–rich countries especially in the areas of economic, commercial and cultural relations.

Secure Sea Lines

To safeguard India's mercantile Marine and sea borne trade in our SLOCs both during peace and war is stated as a naval mission in the Indian Maritime Doctrine. Particularly since the early 1990s, India's trade and energy interests have been expanding far and wide. While this led to the imperative for the navy to acquire extended blue water capabilities, there were severe constraints The UNCLOS–3 also came into force about the same time (1994), which bestowed on India the sovereign rights over an extensive maritime zone. At that time the Indian Coast Guard was still a relatively young service not sufficiently capable to tackle the low–intensity threats in the EEZ. Navy's constabulary role gained greater relevance but this role will now have to be discharged at a greater distance from the shore. Due to Increasing significance of commercial shipping for national development, hence securing sea lines from piracy and maritime terrorism has become prominent peacetime function for Coast Guards and Navies around the world the key choke points of Hormuz Strait, Bab–al–Mandeb and Malacca straits are thus particularly vulnerable. The surveillance and presence of Coast Guard and naval units do provide a measure of security to the sea lines in the northern Indian Ocean. This will be supplemented further south by Hi–tech radar stations being set up by Navy at key locations like Maldives and Madagascar to monitor mercantile traffic Beyond the choke points too, The Navy maintains an occasional presence as a spin off from its foreign port visits and joint exercises with other navies. Securing the vastly extended sea lines would necessitate a prohibitively large number of assets such as major war vessels and frontline surveillance aircrafts/UAV's.

It is important to note that the sea lines transiting the Indian Ocean are of immense significance to many extra regional powers for their energy needs. Of the 200 vessels crossing the Indian Ocean everyday 40 are tankers sourced primarily from Persian Gulf and Africa, the oil and natural gas laden on these tankers are vital to satiate the growing energy appetites of West and East Asian countries. The compulsions of energy security have led Japan and Chinese naval forays into these waters. This implies that the interests of these extra regional states converge with those of India in terms of security of energy sea lines.

Considering the importance of Persian Gulf sea lines for India's energy imports and the fact that this region is just 600nm from Indian shores, India has an important role to play in its maritime security. However as a participant of the Gulf dialogue (which Includes Maritime Security Issues) and through bilateral engagement with the sub regional states, India needs to be continuously involved.

Finally there is a pertinent question for Indian policy makers. In a scenario wherein navigation across Malacca Strait or Strait of Hormuz is impeded due to terrorist action or a military conflict, would the Indian maritime forces be tasked to secure India's vital energy supplies either alone or within coalition of states? It may be necessary to decide upon the responses to such questions in advance if India wishes not to be caught unawares and thus take informed decisions to further its national interests.

Regulate Maritime Zones

Towards achieving 'good order 'in India's maritime zones in terms of combating piracy and other maritime crimes, the foremost imperative is enhanced maritime domain awareness. This needs intensified surveillance at sea and data linking of various government agencies involved, from intelligence agencies and local police to maritime forces. This would enable security forces to compile a common surface picture and thus take informed and timely actions to mitigate the threats. Such domain awareness would need to be backed by patrol forces actually present in the vicinity or readily available at call to interdict the miscreants and act as a deterrence factor.

In the past few years, concerted efforts have been made in this direction, including the augmentation of aerial surveillance of Andaman and Nicobar islands and southern tip of peninsular India through induction of Unmanned Aerial Vehicles, as well as the installation of fixed radar chains and real, time digital data links connecting the Maritime Operation Centers (MOC) with the units at sea. The responsibility for the security of offshore platforms which is essentially a coast guard function continues to rest with the Navy. For this purpose Indian navy has designated an admiral as the Flag–officer Offshore Defence Advisory Group (FODAG), who coordinates the activities of various agencies towards ensuring the security of India's offshore rigs. However irrespective of which is the lead agency for security of the offshore assets, adequate resources would need to be allocated for their security, particularly in terms of underwater surveillance systems.

As in the case of security of sea lines mentioned earlier, interstate security cooperation is essential to regulate the maritime zones. Information exchange with maritime neighbours and coordination of naval patrols is necessary. India has instituted such arrangements with Indonesian and Thai Navy. Owing to these coordinated patrols there has been reported drop in the incidents of piracy in Bay of Bengal. It may also be worthwhile to enter into such arrangements with Myanmar and Bangladesh to regulate India's maritime zone in the northern Bay of Bengal.

Enhance Capacity/Security of Ports and Shipping

The Indian government has initiated some measures to facilitate the inflow of tankers laden with energy resources. The Sagar Mala (Ocean Necklace) project envisaged the development of many ports dotted along the entire Indian peninsula, including facilities for discharging energy resources. However, given the increasing volumes of sea borne trade involving Indian ports, the increase of mercantile traffic may soon outpace these measures and thus advanced technological systems such as Vessel Traffic Management System (VTMS) will need to be installed in the approaches to the ports and areas allocated for tankers.

Security of the ports is very important. It is at present handled by the port operators, whereas the seaward security is the responsibility of the respective coastal states. Considering that the port operations are being privatized, it is very essential for seaward defence to be intensified in various ways, including through the installation of underwater surveillance equipment. The Institution of Marine Police under the jurisdiction of respective states is another positive step to enhance the security along the coast and port areas.

Conclusion

To establish the energy security on a firm footing, the states have been increasingly using and securing their sea routes. India has to see that its economic interests are not attacked to disturb its energy security. Its oil and natural gas resources from its own extensive maritime zones and from overseas imports have to be protected diplomatically and militarily. In any eventuality, India's economic development, which is at its lowest at present, can further deteriorate if oil imports reduce due to any reason thereof.

Governments and agencies, both states and non–state actors, could harm India's vital interests, especially energy lifelines operating through the sea. The conflicts within the Asian countries and the growth of organized pirates take to violent measures including terrorist attacks. Their links with 'Jihadis' operating against India are well established. The terrorists may not yet possess adequate nautical expertise to conduct widespread attacks at sea but achieving this eventually is not outside the bounds of reasonable possibility. Besides the terrorists have strong motivations to overcome the hurdles as demonstrated by 9/11 and 26/11. Their tendency for patient and deliberate planning is well known and their capacities to attack are known beyond doubt.

India has thus to reduce its vulnerabilities with respect to its growing need for fossil fuel resources. National effort in this direction would necessarily include beefing up of country's intrinsic defensive mechanism and attaining self sufficiency of vessels for transporting critical energy resources from abroad as well as those sourced from India's maritime zones. Also necessary is the framing of deliberate policy, in conformity with the regional geopolitical and strategic scenarios, to enhance the capabilities of maritime forces, and to forge security bonds with countries that could facilitate India's efforts towards ensuring its energy security in coming years.

References

1. Ghosh, P K. 2006. The maritime dimensions of India's energy security calculus. Maritime Affairs, Vol 2(1), p 32.

2. Tonnesson, S and Olas, A. 2006. Energy security in Asia : China, India, oil and peace. PRIO Report, IPRI, p 40.

3. Aziz, I, 2006. Gulf oil and India's energy needs. India Strategic. February 1, p 48.

4. Khurana, G S. Security of maritime energy lifelines : policy imperatives for India. In Noronha, Ligia and Sudarshan, Anant, ed. India's energy security. London :Routledge, 2009. p. 87–96.

5. Choudhary, R R. 1998. Energy security policy for India. IDSA Strategic Analysis. February 21, 1998. P 1675

Chapter –9

Renewable Energy in India

The World Energy Forum has predicted that fossil–based oil, coal and gas reserves will be exhausted in less than another ten decades. Fossil fuels account for 79% of the primary energy consumed in the world and 57.5% of that amount is used in the transport sector and are diminishing rapidly. The exhaustion of natural resources and an accelerated demand of conventional energy have forced planners and policy makers to look for alternate source.

Renewable energy is the energy derived from the resources that are regenerative and do not deplete over time. Renewable energy offers our planet a chance to reduce the carbon emissions, cleans the air and put our civilization on a more sustainable footing. It also offers countries around the world the chance to improve their energy security and spur economic development.

Renewable Energy Sources (RES) that use indigenous resources have the potential to provide energy with negligible emissions of air pollutants and greenhouse gases. Renewable Energy Technologies produce marketable energy by converting natural phenomena/ resources into useful energies. The usage of renewable energy resources is a promising prospect for the future as an alternative to conventional energy.

Renewable Energy in India

India's population of more than 1028 million is growing at an annual rate of 1.58%. As fossil fuel energy becomes scarcer, India will face energy shortages significantly due to increase in energy prices and energy insecurity within the next few decades. Increased use of fossil fuels also causes environmental problems both locally and globally. The economy of India measured in USD exchange rate terms is twelfth largest in the world with a GDP of around $1 trillion (2008) with the GDP growth rate of 8%. It is the second fastest big emerging economy, after China, in the world. There is very high demand for energy, which is currently satisfied mainly by coal, foreign oil and petroleum, which apart from being a Non–renewable, and therefore non–permanent solution to the energy crisis, it is imperative that India obtains energy security without affecting the booming economy, which would mean that the country must switch from the non–renewable energy (crude oil and coal) to renewable energy.

Energy is a basic requirement for economic development and in every sector of Indian economy. It is thus necessary that India quickly look towards new and emerging renewable energy and energy efficient technologies as well as implement energy conservation laws. Against this background the country urgently needs to develop a sustainable path of energy development. Promotion of energy conservation and increased use of renewable energy sources are the twin planks of a sustainable energy supply. Fortunately India is blessed with variety of renewable energy sources, like biomass, the solar, the wind, geothermal, and small hydropower and implementing one of the largest programmes in renewable energy. Renewable energy, excluding large hydro projects already account for 9% of the total Installed energy capacity, equivalent to 12,610 MW of energy, in combination with large hydro projects, the capacity is more than 34% i.e 48,643 MW in a total installed capacity of 144.980 MW.

The country has an estimated renewable energy potential of around 85000 MW from commercially exploitable sources i.e wind 45000 MW; small hydro 15000 MW and biomass/bioenergy, 25000 MW. In addition, India has the potential to generate 35 MW per square kilometer using solar photovoltaic and solar thermal energy. There has been a phenomenal progress in wind power and with an installed capacity of over 15700 MW India occupies fifth position globally.

The role of new and renewable energy has been assuming increasing significance in recent times with growing concern for country's energy security. The renewable energy industry has approximately USD 500 million as turnover. The investment being about USD 3 billion. The Indian government has been at work, making a comprehensive policy for compulsory use renewable energy resources through biomass, hydropower, wind, solar and municipal waste in the country, particularly for commercial establishments, as well as Government establishment.

According to the 11th new and renewable energy five year plan from Oct 2008 to 2012 the renewable energy market has reached an estimated US$19 billion. Investments of US $15 billion will be required in order to add to approximately 15000 megawatts (MW) of renewable energy to the present Installed capacity. By the end of 2012 it is expected that renewable energy will contribute 10% of total power generation capacity and have 4–5% share in the electricity mix. This implies that growth in renewable energy will occur at a much faster pace than traditional power generation with renewables making up 20% of the 70000 MW of the total additional energy planned up to 2012. Wind Energy alone is expected to add more than 10000 MW of additional capacity by 2012, followed small hydro 1400 MW co–generation 1200 MW and biomass 500 MW.

Biomass

In recent years, the interest in using biomass as an energy source has increased and it represents approximately 14% of world final energy consumption. Estimates have indicated that 15–50% of the world's primary energy use could come from biomass by the year 2050. The energy obtained from biomass is a form of renewable energy and in principle, utilizing this energy does not add carbon dioxide, a major greenhouse gas, to the atmosphere, in contrast to fossil fuels. As per an estimate, globally photosynthesis produces 220 billion dry tonnes of biomass each year with 1% conversion efficiency. Biomass resources suitable for energy production covers a wide range of materials, from firewood collected in farmlands and natural woods to agriculture and forestry crop grown specifically for energy production purposes. Energy production from food wastes or food processing wastes, especially from waste edible oils, seems to be attractive based on bio–resource sustainability, environmental protection and economic consideration. India is very rich in biomass and has a potential of 16,881(agro–residues and plantations). 5000 MW (bagasse cogeneration) and 2700 MW (energy recovery from waste). Biomass power generation in India is an industry that attracts investments of over 600 crores every year, generating more than 5000 million units of electricity and yearly employment of more than 10 million man days in rural areas.

Hydropower

Hydropower is another source of renewable energy that converts the potential energy or kinetic energy of water into mechanical energy in the form of water mills, textile machines etc, as electrical energy (hydroelectricity generation). It refers to the energy produced from water (rainfall flowing into rivers etc). Hydropower is the largest renewable energy resource being used for the generation of electricity. Only about 17% of the vast hydel potential of 150,000 MW has been tapped so far. Countries like Norway, Canada and Brazil have all been utilizing more than 30% of their hydro potential, while on the other hand India and China have lagged far behind. India ranks fifth in terms of exploitable hydro potential in the world. According to CEA(central electricity authority), India is endowed with economically exploitable hydropower potential to the tune of 148,700 MW. The dominant annual rainfall is located on the North Eastern part of India:Arunachal Pradesh, Assam, Nagaland, Manipur and Mizoram, and also on west coast between Mumbai and Mahe. Primary hydroelectric power plants are located in Bihar, Punjab, Uttrakhand, Karnataka, Uttar Pradesh, Sikkim, Jammu & Kashmir, Gujarat, and Andhra Pradesh. In India, hydropower projects with station capacity of up to 25 (MW) fall under the category of small hydropower (SHP). India has an estimated SHP potential of about 15,000 MW, of which about 11% has been tapped so far. The Ministry of New and Renewable Energy (MNRE) supports SHP project development throughout the country. So far, 523 SHP projects with an aggregate capacity of 1705 MW area under implementation. With a capacity addition on an average, of 100 MW per year and gradual decrease in gestation periods and capital costs, the SHP sector is becoming increasingly competitive with other alternatives. Some key figures concerning small hydro in India:

- Less than 25 MW is in the small hydro designation   4096 potential sites have been identified.

- There is potential of 15000 MW   Technology is mature and reliable.

- Installed is 1520 MW to date

two types of technology are used.

(I) High–head systems.

(II) Low– head systems.

Wind Energy

Winds are generated by complex mechanisms involving the rotation of the earth, heat energy from the sun, the cooling effects of the oceans and polar ice caps, temperature gradients between land and sea and the physical effects of the mountains and other obstacles. Wind is widely distributed energy resource. Total world wind capacity at the end of 2006 was around 72000 MW. Wind energy is being developed in the industrialsed world for environmental reason and it has attractions in the developing world as it can be installed quickly in areas where electricity is urgently needed. In many instances it may be cost effective solution if fossil fuel sources are not readily available. In addition there are many applications for wind energy in remote regions worldwide, either for supplementing diesel power (which tends to be expensive) or for supplying farms, homes and other installations on an individual basis.

The availability of wind varies for different regions. Wind resources can be exploited mainly in areas where wind power density is at least 400 W/M Sq at 30 m above the ground, India's wind energy potential has been assessed at 46000 MW. A capacity of 8757 MW up to 31 Mar 2008 has so far been added through wind, The Wind Power program in India was initiated towards the end of the sixth plan in 1983–84.

India is surpassed only by Germany as one of the world's fastest growing markets for wind energy. There is an installed capacity of 5310 MW however ten times the potential of 46000 MW exists. Different types of Wind Power Generators used in India for Off grip power generation ie water pumping windmills, aero–generators (a small wind electric generator having a capacity of up to 30 KW) and wind solar hybrid systems.

Solar Energy

Solar energy is the abundant permanent energy resource on the earth and it is available for use in its direct (solar radiation) and indirect (Wind, Biomass, Hydro, Ocean, etc) forms. Solar energy experienced by us as heat and light, can be used through two routes : The thermal route uses the heat for water heating, cooking, drying, water purification, power generation, and other applications : the photovoltaic route converts the light in solar energy into electricity, which can then be used for a number of purposes such as lighting, pumping, communications, and power supply in an electrified areas.

The total annual solar radiation falling on the earth is more than 7500 times the world's total annual primary energy consumption of 450 EJ. The annual solar radiation reaching the earth's surfacei.e approximately 3,400,000 EJ, is an order of magnitude greater than all the estimated (discovered and undiscovered) nonrenewable energy resources including fossil fuels and nuclear. Most parts of India receive 4–7 KWh of solar radiation per square meter per day with 250–300 sunny days in a year. The highest annual radiation energy is received in western Rajasthan while the North–Eastern region of the country receives the lowest annual radiation. India has a good level of solar radiation, receiving the solar energy equivalent of more than 5000 trillion KWh/year. Depending on the location, the daily incidence ranges from 4 to7 KWh/sq m, with the hours of sunshine ranging from 2300 to 3200 per year.

The Prime Minister released the National Action Plan on climate change (NAPCC) on 30th June, 2008. The plan proposes to start 8 missions, amongst which one is the National Solar Mission. Solar thermal and Solar Photovoltaic are both encompassed by the Solar Energy Programme that is being implemented by Ministry (Regarded as one of the largest in the world.) to utilize India's estimated solar power potential of 20 and 35 MW/sq km solar thermal. India's overall potential for solar water heating system has been estimated to be 140 million sq meter of collector area. Solar air heating technology has been applied to various industrial and agricultural processes (e.g drying/curing, regeneration of dehumidifying agents, timber seasoning, leather tanning) and also for space heating : many types of solar dryers have been developed for use in different situations. Solar buildings have been promoted by the MNRE in an effort to increase energy efficiency. The Solar Photovoltaic Program (SPV) promoted by the ministry for the past two decades ,has been aimed particularly at rural and remote areas. Following the success of the country wide SPV demonstration and utilization program during the period of ninth and tenth plan, it is planned with certain modifications, to continue it during the eleventh plan.

Geothermal Energy

Geothermal is the energy generated from heat stored in the earth or the collection of absorbed heat derived from underground. Immense amount of Thermal energy is generated and stored in the Earth's core, mantle and crust. Geothermal energy is at present contributing about 10000mw over the world and India's small resources can augment the above percentage. Studies carried out by geological survey of India have observed existence of about 340 hot springs in the country. These are distributed in seven geothermal provinces, the provinces, although found along the west coast in Gujarat and Rajasthan and along a west south west–east– northeast line running from the west coast to the western border of Bangladesh (known as SONATA), are most prolific in the 1500 km stretch of Himalayas. The resource is little used at the moment but the Government has the plan to more than double the current total installed generating capacity in 2012.

Other Renewable Energy Technologies

Solar thermal technologies, particularly solar water heating system, solar cookers and solar generation systems are the most commercialized technologies among renewable energy technologies in India. Policies are set to provide further impetus to dissemination of solar technologies.

Biogas represents an alternative source of energy,derived mainly from organic waste , primarily cow dung has been promoted for over three decades now. Biogas is a clean fuel produced through anaerobic digestion of variety of organic waste: animal, agricultural domestic and industrial. Biogas is the only technology that has put cooking in rural areas on technological ladder and has made cooking a pleasure with associated social and environmental benefits including zero indoor pollution. India's National Project on bio-gas development (NPBD) has been one of the well organized and systematic program to provide logistic and institutional support for that has been under implementation since early 1980s. The ultimate goal of this program is to set up bio-gas plants in around 12 million households that have enough cattle to maintain a regular supply of dung.

Hydrogen energy is also at early stage of development. Ministry of New and Renewable Energy also funded research projects on different aspects of hydrogen energy technology development .The road map envisages taking up of research ,development and demonstration activities in various sectors of hydrogen energy technologies and visualized goals of one million hydrogen fuelled vehicles and 1000 MW aggregate hydrogen based power generation capacity to be set up in the country by 2020.

Future of Renewable Energy in India

India faced with twin challenges on energy and environmental front, has no option but to work towards increasing the role of renewable in the future energy system. Renewable energy technologies vary widely in their technological maturity and commercial status. In India renewable energy is at a take off stage and businesses. Industry government and customer have a large number of issues to address before these technologies could make a real penetration. India with large renewable energy resources (Solar PV, wind, solar Heating ,small hydro and biomass)is to set to have large scale development and deployment of renewable energy projects. The aim of meeting 10%of the country power supply through renewable by 2012 and also ambitious plans for the distribution of biogas plants solar PV application and solar city appears to be within reach.

India would also have to look for international cooperation in Renewable energy through well–defined R & D projects with proper division of labour and responsibilities for specific tasks with equitable financial burden and credit sharing arrangements. Renewable energy development is considered in India to be of great importance from the point of view of long term energy supply security, environmental benefits and climate change mitigation. The integrated energy policy report has recognized the need maximally develop domestic supply option as well as the need to diversify the energy sources. It is expected that the contribution from renewables in power generation alone can be to the extent of 60000 MW in the year 2031–2032. A modest assessment in the renewable energy sector will be about Rs 300,000 crores over the next 25 years. MNRE has included in its mission : energy security; increase in the share of clean power : energy availability and access; energy affordability: and energy equity.

Conclusion

Energy security, economic growth and environmental protection are the national energy policy drivers of any country of the world. The need to boost the efforts for further development and promotion of renewable energy resources has been felt world over in the light of high prices of the crude oil. A critical part of the solution will lie in promoting renewable energy technologies as a way to address the concerns about energy security, economic growth in the face of rising energy prices, competitiveness,include promoting deployment, innovation and basic research in renewable energy technologies resolving the barriers to health costs and environmental degradation. Specific action point that has been mentioned include promoting deployment, innovation and basic research in renewable energy technologies resolving the barriers to development and commercial deployment of biomass, hydropower, solar and wind technologies, promoting straight biomass combustion and biomass gasification technologies, promoting the development and manufacture of small wind electric generators. Accordingly increased focus is being laid on the deployment of renewable power that is likely to account for around 5% in the electricity–mix by 2032. Finally renewable energy provides enormous benefits and can contribute significantly in the national energy mix at least economic, environmental and social costs and it is expected that the share of renewable energy in the total generation capacity will increase in future.

References

1. International Energy Agency, Key world energy statistics available at http// www.iea.org/ Text basefree/ /nppdf/key2006.pdf.

2.   World energy outlook, International energy agency :2008 http//www. World energy outlook .org /2008.asp.

3.   REN21, Renewables 2007global status report http://www.ren21 .net /pdf/

4.   REN21 ,renewable 2009 global status report http:/www. ren 21.com.

5.   VarunaSK,Singal Review of augmentation of energy needs using renewable energy sources in India .

6.   Planning Commission , Government of India–September 1995 and SEP1996 projections to 2020–2021.

7.   Subramanium V. renewable energy : status and future prospects. MNRE 2007

8.   GOI, tenth five year plan 2002–2007,Planning Commission. New Delhi available at http://planning commission .nic .in / about us committee

9.   Urjaakshay newsletter of Ministry of Renewable Energy Government of India Oct 2008.

10. India 2009 , energy publication division, Ministry of Information & Broadcasting, Government of India :2009.

11. KPMG, India energy outlook 2007.

12. UrjaAkshayNewsletter of the Ministry of new and Renewable Government of India Dec 2008.

13. Ghosh D Shukla, PR Garg, A Rammana , Renewable energy technologies for the Indian power sector : mitigation potential and operational strategies. Renewable and strategic energy reviews.

14. Conn1 energy trends and technologies for the coming decades. Address to the Harvard university centre.

15. Maithani PC Renewable energy policy framework of India . Narosa publication delhi.

16. Ashwanikumar ,kapilkumar , Nareshkaushik ,Satyavatisharma, Saroj Mishra: Renewable energy in India current status and future potential.

Chapter –10

Energy Security and Climate Change

Energy security and climate change are amongst the most serious concerns for many developing countries. Counties are now trying to reduce energy demand to mitigate climate change risks through efforts targeted at various sectors of the economy, for instance increasing energy efficiency and enforcing conservation measures in industry and service sectors ; using alternate fuels in the transport sector ; reducing electricity usage in the agricultural sector ; and so on. They are also paying attention at the household level. It is important to bear in mind that personal consumption at the household level is inseparably connected with energy use, emission of GHGs (greenhouse gases) and thus climate change.

Changes in lifestyles and consumption patterns can immensely contribute to improving energy security and mitigating climate change. The recommended changes in this regard, in effect boil down to the choices that we make, in everyday lives, for instance, what food we buy, the way we cook, and the modes of transport we use.

The developed countries have been historically responsible for high levels of consumption and emission. and account the use of most of the ecological space. According to (World Wild Life Fund), an average citizen requires 10 hectares of planet to support his or her lifestyle, while an average European needs over five hectares. An average person in Africa needs about one hectare of the earth to live. When compared to the rest of the world US households accounts for over six times more Carbon Dioxide emissions than the remainder of the world per year on an average. But what is of concern is that with the growth in the population, urbanization and globalization, the per capita energy consumption and emissions from the more affluent segment in the developing countries are gradually converging towards those recorded in the developed countries. For instance, in the past few decades, gains in the household income and urban development in many countries in Asia have led to significant shift in the household use of fuels away from traditional biomass–based household fuels to modern fossil fuels. There is also evidence of dramatic increase in the electricity consumption. These changes clearly demonstrate an improvement in the living conditions but their long term implication for energy consumption and atmospheric emissions are troubling.

Lifestyle changes are not easily achievable as it is difficult to change the mind sets of the people, even if the recommended actions do not involve any significant compromise on comfort. Also changes in peoples lifestyles and the switch to energy–efficient products, can't be forced on consumers. Therefore it becomes extremely difficult to restrict energy use at homes purely through mechanisms. When governments talk about securing Energy at the national level, sectors other than house hold sectors are targeted more, when the household sector should be priority sector targeted by the government since much of the activity in the industrial and commercial sector exists as a response to consumer demands for goods and services. It is evident that with betterment in living conditions, lifestyles lead by the relatively affluent household in the developing countries will add to global energy insecurity and climate change concerns.

The Problem of Converging Lifestyles

The comparison is between the OECD and NON OECD countries. For the non–OECD region as a whole, real GDP is projected to grow by more than 5% per year on an average from 2004 through 2030, population by 1% per year and household energy use is projected grow at a robust rate of 2.4% per year. This is because higher income will foster increased use of energy– using appliances. As a result households in the non–OECD are projected to consume about 10% more energy than households in OECD nations in 2030. China and India are expected to account for more than 40% increase in the residential energy use in the non OECD countries, as their economies continue to grow rapidly over the projection period. By 2030 the non–OECD countries consumption will constitute about 53% of the global residential sector's energy consumption This is indicative of the converging lifestyles of the relatively affluent section in the developing countries with that in the developed countries.

It is evident that the per capita emission levels in the developing countries are still far below that in the developed countries. For instance, the figure for India is 0.05 times that of the US and 0.16 times that of Japan. China is 0.16 times that of US and 0.16 times that of Japan. It shows that as far as carbon dioxide emissions are concerned. China is close to reaching the and India has reached Japan's levels. However, emission levels in East Asian countries like Thailand and Indonesia are much less though the per capita emissions in these countries are higher than the South Asian economies like India. Total energy consumption in these countries is projected to grow at about 3% per annum till 2020.(IEA 2004)

A wide variation can be seen in the overall per capita carbon dioxide emissions of the countries, However the contribution of the particular sector varies significantly across countries. For instance the share of residential sector carbon dioxide emissions per capita in overall per capita emission is higher in India, Indonesia, and Korea as compared to the US or even Japan. Again, the per capita electricity consumption figures shows wide variation. This is primarily because a large fraction of the population in some of the developing countries does not have access to the electricity. For instance, in India only about 43% of the rural population has access to electricity. Similarly in Indonesia, merely 55% of the population enjoys electricity in their homes. But an average person in Indonesia enjoys a better lifestyle than in India and therefore register higher per capita emission. The same is true for Thailand where figures for electricity access are better and the per capita emission level is higher. In China close to 100% of the population has the access to electricity but owing to the high population, the per capita usage is much less. In Korea the per capita emission is just about half of that in US but it has a population which is only 16% of that of the US. The per capita carbon dioxide emissions of the residential sector in Korea are higher than that in Japan, Though the per capita electricity consumption is not much less than Japan. In the years to come with accelerating development, urbanization and population growth, coupled with better electricity access overall per capita energy consumption and emission including those from the residential sector are projected to rise faster.

Imapact of Lifestyle on Energy Consumption and Emission from the Household Sector in Select Asian Countries

India

India is home to two contradictory realities. On one hand there is a rapidly growing rich consumer class, which has made the country the 12th largest luxury market in the world. On the other, about 57% of rural India does not have access to electricity, firewood and wood chips continued to be the most important sources of energy for cooking in rural India, with 75% of the rural households' dependent upon them. In the urban sector kerosene 10%, firewood and chips 22% and LPG 57% are important sources of energy used for cooking. Also, electricity and kerosene together served 99% of the households as primary source for lighting in both rural and urban areas. Between 2000 and 2008 there has been an increase in the proportion of household using electricity for lighting purpose, by 7% (from 48% to 55%) in rural areas and by 3% in urban India. The residential sector in India accounted for about 25% of sect oral electricity consumption in 2008. Conversion to modern fuels has added to the increased energy use per capita of the households.

A green peace report says that the richest consumer class in India produces 4.5 times more carbon dioxide than the poorest class, While even the rich Indians still have half the carbon footprint of an average European, they have reached the global average. The relatively rich consumer section uses all kinds of modern electronic devices. High energy consumption and emissions from the richer section of the population is offset by low energy use and emissions from the poorer section, resulting in overall low per capita energy use and emissions.

As far as demand for transportation is concerned consumption of petrol and diesel grew at 7.3% and 5.8% per annum respectively between 1980 and 2005 (planning commission 2006). This is the outcome of the growth of personal motorized transport and the rise in the share of road haulage due to an increase in urban sprawl. With improving income and changing lifestyle, many can now afford a car. As a result the automobile industry, increased at an average particularly the small car segment is booming. The number of cars , jeeps and taxis has increased at an average annual growth rate of

10% whereas the two wheelers have shown the highest average annual growth rate of 14% during the period 1980–2006. According to the EIA (Energy Information Administration), India is expected to show the largest increase in transportation sector energy consumption among the Non–OECD countries. The combined growth rate for transportation energy use in all the countries of central and south American economies is projected to be similar to that in India. This could have serious implications for the country's energy security.

The construction sector in India too is growing rapidly. Though the construction sector in India includes industrial constructions, roads, ports and other infrastructure, it is in real estate (both residential and commercial) that the maximum investment is directed. There is a significant demand for quality housing in India. With younger people wanting to own a house, owing to the greater affordability due to reasonable interest rates on home loans and favorable tax treatment. The demand for residential housing is expected to continue to grow in the near future. However construction activities in India have been pursued without attention to environmental issues. Construction material used are energy intensive and there is a scope for the use of the appropriate materials and designs that can save energy, both in construction and use (Air conditioning and lighting are the two most energy consuming end uses in the building sector.) At the national level, domestic and commercial buildings account for more than 30% of annual electricity consumption.

In order to reduce energy consumption of the household sector, the following action points on demand side management were agreed upon by Bureau of Energy Efficiency

- Bulk procurement and distribution of CFLs.

- Adopting of ECBC (energy conservation building code.)

- Promotion and mandating of the use of Energy efficient pumps and other energy efficient appliances.

The scheme on CFLs seeks to replace an estimated 400 million incandescent bulbs with CFLs which could save 6000 MW to 10000 MW of power. It seeks to make available high quality CFLs at the cost of incandescent bulbs. The basic premise for the second and third action point is to create the appropriate legal and regulatory environment for energy–efficient end use products and to provide consumer with options to make an informed choice. The plan aims to reduce overall energy consumption by 3000 MW by the end 2012.

China

In China, overall emissions are quite high because of the large population size but energy requirements vary significantly within the country due to different weather conditions, indoor environment, residence type and lifestyle of the region. In rural China, large quantities of biomass fuel such as stalks and firewood are used for cooking and space heating. In urban areas, biomass is not used. Nevertheless, lifestyle differences between rural and urban residents are gradually reducing. In rural regions commercial energy sources such as coal, oil, electricity and natural gas are becoming popular and affordable, and this is gradually substituting the use of noncommercial energy sources such as straw and firewood. The most energy–intensive residents' behavior is the use of direct energy, followed by food, education, cultural and recreational services and personal travel.

Consumer behavior in urban China is following that of developed countries. In the automobile segment, bigger cars are more popular. Excessive air conditioning and heating are not uncommon. Economic reforms have resulted in considerable improvements in people's quality of life, with large section of society experiencing a transition out of poverty to the western lifestyles. Of the increase in carbon dioxide emissions due to household consumption, followed by a strong growth in many service sectors such as education real estate and restaurants. Increased use of computers, refrigerators, television sets and air conditioners. The number of air conditioners in use has significantly to about 30 sets per 100 households. The popularization of household electronics has enormously boosted household appliance production. A recent study suggests that approximately 26% of total energy consumption and 30% of carbon dioxide emissions in china every year are a consequences residents lifestyles, and economic activities that support these demands.

South Korea

The Korean household sector was responsible for about 52% of the national primary energy requirements in the period from 1980 to 2000. Households continue to consume more and more electricity intensive goods & services. A survey undertaken as part of the study reveals that the energy consumed per household and per person is 2.341 TOE and 0.639 TOE respectively.

South Korea has long winters ,and energy use for heating comprises a big proportion of total energy consumed . The energy consumption household under different heads was found from the survey, is 0.415 TOE for heating water, 1.490 TOE for heating space, 0.307 TOE for lighting and 0.131 TOE for cooking. With rapid urbanization, city gas grids too have been expanding rapidly and gas is now the dominant cooking fuel.

Korea's energy consumption for transport is dominated by the road transport sub sector, representing more than 75% of the economy's total transport energy consumption. Over the past two decades, income growth, improving in living standards, expansion of residential suburbs and development of vehicle manufacturing industries, have all contributed to thirty fold increase in in the stock of vehicles, which has in turn resulted in tenfold increase in gasoline and diesel consumption.

The KEMCO (Korean Energy management corporation) is a nonprofit government agency in charge of implementing energy efficiency and conservation policies in the country. KEMCO launched the energy efficiency standards and Labeling Program to eliminate inefficient designs from the market and help consumers choose more energy efficient goods which grade the energy efficiency from 1to 5. This program covers electric refrigerators, air conditioners, incandescent lamp, fluorescent lamps and self–ballasted lamps and passenger cars. It is applied both to domestic products and imported products.

Japan

Since 1990, Japanese household emissions have gone up nearly 40%. Some of the Japan's environmental experts attribute this rise to increasing consumerism. Consumer behavior thus holds the key to Japan's ability to fulfill its commitments under the 1997 Kyoto Protocol.

Japan is a country where energy consciousness is quite high. In 2005, the government introduced a national campaign, urging Japanese to replace their older appliances and buy hybrid vehicles, all part of tremendous effort to save energy to fight global warming. In April 2005 The Global Warming Prevention Headquarters led by the government, launched a large scale national campaign called team minus 6%. The campaign aims to have individuals businesses and other organization work together to achieve a 6% reduction in GHG emissions. In particular, it calls on people to

- Set air conditioners at 28 degree Celsius 9(Temperature Control)

- Avoid wasting water at taps (wise use of water)

- Choose and buy energy efficient eco–friendly products (green purchasing)

- Stop car idling (smart driving) Say no to excessive packaging. (waste reduction)

- Unplug devices when they are not being used. (wise use of electricity)

In addition, business–wear fashions called Cool Biz (during summer) and Warm Biz(during winters help office workers adapt to set room temperatures. Engaged in this energy conservation program any companies have reported large savings on electricity bill. Also Japan's top runner program in the commercial and transport sector has realized a substantial improvement in energy efficiency. The program sets the fuel efficiency standards higher than the performance of the best product commercially available in the product category. Manufacturers who do not meet the standards are given advice, publicaly announced, given an order, or fined. The energy saving labeling system has also been introduced in Japan to inform consumers of the efficiency of home appliances and promote energy efficient products.

Conclusion

Affluent households of key Asian countries are following lifestyle similar to those in the developed countries, and are becoming highly energy intensive . A study of developing Asian countries shows that though the per capita energy consumption and emissions in these countries still well below the world average, with development, growth in population, urbanization, and changing lifestyles, energy consumption by, and emissions from the relatively affluent sections of the house hold sector are increasing fast and will soon reach the levels observed in the developed countries. This will have significant impact on energy security and climate.

Making individuals aware of the problem is important, so that they recognize their role in formulating solutions, and voluntarily adjust their personal consumption. Also it is noticed that even though awareness and concern about energy security and climate is widespread in some cases. These are rarely translated into consistent and adequate action. This calls for the spread ideas and initiatives, and the design of widespread action plans. Countries need to exchange information on best practices in policy design and implementation. Possible action points include the following.

- More incentives should be put in place to encourage consumers to choose energy saving products and services.

- Consumer should be informed of impact of their choices and actions, and the possible ways reducing their carbon footprint.

- The use of energy conservation technology should be encouraged.

- Regulation by stipulating energy usage or standardizing a quota should be introduced by the government to facilitate right consumer choices.

References

1.   APEC(Asia Pacific Economic Cooperation)2006

2.   Improving consumer lifestyle choices key to meeting carbon dioxide goals.

The Japan times, 28 April 2007.

3. Lim K C and Kang YY. Analysis of the effects of lifestyles on the Energy consumption of the household sector.

4. Miki.T.:Energy efficiency and conservation policy in Japan.

5. NSSO(national sample survey organization) Energy sources of Indian households for cooking and lighting.

6. Mitali Das Gupta. Energy Security and climate change : why we should be concerned with the converging lifestyles.

7. Park Hand Hoe. E : The direct and indirect household energy requirements in the Republic of Korea : an input–output analysis.

8. Planning Commission 2006 : Integrated energy policy.

9. Implementing End use Efficiency Improvements in India : Drawing from experience in the US and other countries.

Chapter –11

Policy Recommendations

In order to chalk out the plans for the energy security preparedness, it is very pivotal that a holistic view is taken into consideration. The stringent policies needs to be in place to introduce a new thinking into the system which will strengthen the India's energy security scenario. The government and various other agencies must consider it on their topmost agenda so that the policies are drafted and the work gets initiated.

Nuclear policy

- There is a need to harmonize our narratives on nuclear nonproliferation and develop a frame work that is equitable harmonious and sustainable.

- There is a need to open the market to private players, foreign companies and to have joint ventures with foreign utilities. Opening the field to the private sector will necessitate lot of legislative and policy changes.

- Need to understand public perceptions on nuclear energy, which should be considered integral to nuclear power development.

Hydropower

- A committee of intellectuals along with some key representatives from other stake holder groups must be formed and only after gaining acceptance from such a committee should the construction of dam be initiated.

- Compensation packages for those displaced and affected should be such that the people after relocation can live a better life. Laws to safeguard and security of these displaced people needs to be enacted and made mandatory for the decision makers and planners of the large dams.

- Need to go in for smaller dams than large scale dams.

- Treaties are the best way to deal with disputes and differences over interstate hydropower projects.

Renewable Energy

- The government in India needs to encourage generation facilities based on biomass with captive plantations since this is the only renewable resources as of now that can generate power on 24×7 basis.

- An aggressive policy to absorb the solar power as it is generated needs to be put in place. This would obviate the need for storage and reduce costs significantly

- Government support for lowering the cost of loan s to start up solar power projects

- There is a need to revisit the institutional arrangements, business models, role of government as well as private sector in developing the market for biomass

- Incentives to develop renewable energy sector need to be adjusted as the market develops

- Subsidies to support the renewable energy sector should not last forever. This is required to ensure that renewable energy becomes a commercially viable sector. There is a requirement to develop innovative financing mechanisms for MAKING RENEWABLE ENERGY SUSTAINABLE AND COMMERCIALLY VIABLE.

General Recommendations

Timely Investments

The problem today is not as much about the availability of oil in the future but of timely investments. Even if there is not enough conventional oil, there is enough unconventional oil, which requires timely investments by both producers as well as consumers.

Technology Innovation For Less Carbon Intensity

- While the world has to move away from a more carbon–

intensive future, the fact is that the fossil fuels will remain the main source of energy for country like India. Therefore the real option lies in adopting certain technologies that would help cut down emissions from the use of fossil fuels. Producers and consumers have to collectively develop innovative energy technology options.

- Moving towards a more carbon constrained future will require a policy framework that will have to incorporate structural reforms, both internationally as well as within countries.

Foreign Policy Propositions

- India has expanded its search for hydrocarbon assets around the world as part of its national objective. This has required large scale investments by public and private sector. Equity oil has thus become a strategic necessity. The dependence on equity oil in countries, often some of the most fragile in the world today, brings with it a reliance on a range of new diplomatic instruments. These should include the development of nontraditional instruments of influence on the ruling elites, and increased stakes in the stability of particular regimes in other countries.

- Since the nuclear tests of 1998, gaining access to international cooperation in atomic energy has consumed much of India's diplomatic energies Renewed global interests in nuclear power amidst rising oil prices and concerns of global warming appears to have confirmed India's enduring faith in nuclear power as an important alternative. However to regain access to international nuclear energy markets India has needed to restructure its decade old organization of its national nuclear programme as well as undertake legal obligation on non–proliferation. India will have to demonstrate support for nonproliferation with other nuclear powers. It will also need to adjust policies to defend the global nuclear order.

- 'The search for energy security has begun to redefine India's relation with great powers. Energy security dialogue between India and the US goes beyond the nuclear question and encompasses a much wider agenda that includes military coordination in protection of sea lanes. Europe, Japan and Russia with their new found importance in global energy market has also emerged at the top of India's energy diplomacy.

* As India's dependencies rise, so must the attention it pays to the balance of power in regions such as the Persian Gulf and central Asia and general improvement of relations in the area. Strategic concerns must be at the forefront.

References

1. Key Challenges, Opportunities and Recommendations: resource security: The Governance Dimension

2. Energy, Security and Indian Foreign Policy : C.Raja Mohan

Bibliography

Ailawadi, V S and Bhattacharyya, S C. Access to energy services by the poor in India : current situation and need for alternative strategies. Natural Resource Forum, 30, 2006, pp 2–14.

Alhaji A F., The meaning of energy security USAEE Blog (http/blog.usaee. org /q-node)2 A quest for energy security in 21stcentury ; Resources and constraints-A paper from Asia Pacific Energy Centre (APERC) 2007.

Andreas, K. Regional disparities in electrification of India–do geographic factors matter ? CPCE Working Paper 51, Zurich : Centre for Energy Policy and Economics, 2006.

A European strategy for sustainable, competitive and secure energy- A Green Paper by European commission.

Barnes, D and Floor, W. Rural energy in developing countries : a challenge for economic development. Annual review of Energy and the Environment. Vol 21, 1996, pp 497–530.

BohiToman D.R. , Energy security : externalities and policies.

BohiToman D.R. , Economics of Energy Security.

Chester Lynne, Does the polysemic nature of energy security make it a wicked problem- a paper presented during during International conference on Energy, Environment and Sustainable Development.

EIA. 2007. Country Analysis Briefs : Persian Gulf Region.

ICFI World Socialist Website.

Marquina A., Energy Security:Visions from Asia and Europe – A Paper

Muller Kranner, Energy Security: Re-measuring the world – A paper

Pachuari, S. An energy analysis of household consumption : changing patterns of direct and indirect use in India. The Netherlands : Springer, 2007.

Pachuari, S, Mueller, A, Kemmler, AandSpreng, D. On measuring energy poverty in Indian households. World Development. Vol 32(12), 2004, pp 2083–2104.

Parikh, J K, Biswas, H and Karmakar, S. Cooking with bio–fuels : risk factors affecting health impact on rural women. Economic and Political Weekly, 2003, pp 2681–2692.

Raja Mohan. C, Energy, Security and Indian Foreign Policy

Saghir, J. Energy and Poverty. Paper presented for the International Energy Forum. Washington, D C : The World Bank, 2004.

Statistical Review of World Energy. British Petroleum.

World Energy Assessment: Energy and Challenge of Sustainability – United Nations Development Progromme2000.

World Economic Forum, The New Energy Security Paradigm -energy vision update.

www.ingramcontent.com/pod-product-compliance
Lightning Source LLC
Chambersburg PA
CBHW070927270326
41927CB00011B/2755